THE PARADOX OF SUCCESS

THE PARADOX OF SUCCESS:

17 STEPS FOR TAKING THE SPOTLIGHT

By Robert Ingelaere

Coauthor: Ling-Chih

Copyright © 2020 Robert Ingelaere, Ling-Chih Sirchia

All rights reserved.

ISBN: 9798654797896

Robert Ingelaere:

I dedicate this book to Bertrand Canavy,

Business partner, friend, and traveling brother.

A special thought to Michèle Sénéchal,

A beautiful person who knows the paradox.

Ling-Chih:

To Dr. Hong Tao-Tze,

to whom I owe the teaching for life.

To my parents, up there or down here,

who have always stood by me.

GENESIS OF THIS BOOK

By Ling-Chih

- ***It all starts with the castle***

I met Robert in 2016 for the first time in a castle where he was organizing Network Marketing distributor meetings, following an invitation from a friend, a great internet marketing enthusiast. This networking evening generated links that were forged as I evolved in Network Marketing. Some got closer, others got further apart. Following this meeting with the great marketer, I reconnected three years later, here I am now co-writing a book on the theme of successful entrepreneurs, based on Robert's experience, and with ... Robert himself.

Robert travels frequently, which means that we sometimes have to work at a distance, with time differences. Today, we are at the end of the writing process, and we are happy to present you this four-handed book, revealing the secrets of the top leaders in Network Marketing.

• *A great authentic leader*

I have the honor of working with Robert for business coaching, and benefiting directly and indirectly from his teaching. The man has impressed me with his charisma, his frankness and his "straight to the *point*", as Americans say. I was able to see with my own eyes what a top international leader, an experienced entrepreneur, is all about. Robert has a presence, and after a few minutes of discussion, you quickly feel that you have the richness of decades of work in the field in front of you.

Robert captivates me with his journey! After hearing a few anecdotes from his life, having a very great visual sensitivity, images popped into my mind. It was an excellent sign! It indicated to me that I needed to dig deeper. As a writer too, I felt that there was material and enormous potential for an atypical story or life journey.

Robert came from nothing and made it to the top. That's mainly due to his psychology and his focus:

1. How did he do it?
2. What did he do to succeed?
3. What else did he do? (or less?)
4. Who makes him a successful entrepreneur?

I am confident that this book will help you recognize the best opportunities, just like the mentor who guided his or her first steps towards a successful career.

Considering the amount of money Robert has raised over the years, I thought I'd meet someone who'd be smug. Well, I was wrong. On the contrary, he's surprisingly approachable, yet very discreet. What surprised me the most was his energy, his passion, and the sincere attention he pays to people. It is not at all "artificial", nor is it something that can be simulated for a very long time. It fits in perfectly with what he says in the book: being a top salesman also means passing on his passion.

Thanks to this meeting, I am aware that this is an incredible opportunity and I am grateful for it. Sometimes in life, destinies intersect. People come and go in and out of our lives. The important thing is not to have someone who accompanies us to the end - even if we want to - because we can't know what the future holds for us. For me it is, after all, to be able to evolve and move forward. The journey is more important than the destination.

- ***The man behind the contractor***

While writing this book, I was often asked a question: what is your book about? Most of the time I gave the classic answer: "It's a book about entrepreneurship, based on Robert Ingelaere's 40 years of experience." However, for a book dedicated to Robert, this answer bears little resemblance to him. Why is that? Because for an average person, to stand out from the crowd is difficult, and the competition is tough in marketing. This description seems to fit the clichés in every way, and to have made all the mistakes in positioning. Above all, I had the impression that I wasn't giving the real answer and that I was only delivering half the reality.

Yes, at first glance, it's a book about entrepreneurship. But for a book about Robert's teaching, you can't decode the message out of context. My first intention was to make a biography, since the quality of a leader is discretion, we decided to make a collection of ideas and advice.

During the writing process, I sometimes wondered about the usefulness of this book: what is our unique offering among a huge quantity of books on entrepreneurship? Could this book contribute to the world and make it a better place? Of course, I don't doubt Robert's excellence, and I would like to find that special touch, especially since I know it's already there, I just have to **REVEAL** it.

That question was in my mind, and it was during this period of the coronavirus epidemic, when I would be shutting myself away at home like millions of people, that the answer came to me.

That answer is **love**. In the face of death, love carries all its meaning.

Robert survived three serious illnesses that almost cost him his life. He suffered betrayals, separations, and tears. As you and I, you might say. Yet he made a choice to deliver only positive and useful experiences, instead of regretting the difficult parts. He turned his back on everything that had hurt him, with the elegance of a leader. He learned from his mistakes, to keep moving forward.

Not everyone has this elegance, at the cost of a total let go.

And that is why I consider that to deliver these experiences is not insignificant: without his perseverance, his iron will, without his deep love for life, he would have given up, and we would never have heard that voice.

To hold out until the end, as long as there is a glimmer of hope, that is the Robert I know, and together we would like to share these messages.

This awareness makes me understand that **your own being is something that nobody teaches you,** but happens **inside you. Nobody offers you your position in life**. You have to find it yourself.

This book is for those who want to succeed, and also for entrepreneurs who are looking to find their way in marketing with like-minded partners. If this is your case, we'll give you tips that have worked for many entrepreneurs. No matter where you are, we want to give you wings. If that's what you're looking for, then you've come to the right place. I invite you to also to discover my co-author, a survivor, an enthusiast, a passionate. A talent.

SUCCESS IS A STATE OF MIND

By Robert Ingelaere

The marketing sector has evolved a lot, like a typical system that is changing. Sales have also evolved a lot, with different approaches and tools accompanying this transformation.

As an experienced marketer, I am about to gradually transform the complicated system and expose the seemingly complex model into a typical concept easily understandable by anyone who wants to take advantage of network sales and marketing.

I've been working in sales and marketing for 40 years. I've known the pros and cons in these fields, and I fully understand what it feels like to start from scratch, from a very modest level and then climb up the ladder one by one to become famous.

I started at the bottom, many years ago. I had a very complicated start in life, losing my parents at an early age. I was raised by my grandparents, and at the time we were living very modestly with my grandfather's retirement as a miner. As soon as I reached working age, at 16, I dropped out of school and went to the factory with my brother to help my family. It was hard work, but that's what got us into the refrigerator.

But marketing doesn't necessarily have to be done in a difficult way to work, there are concepts called "Network

Marketing" and "Law of Attraction" to be followed like a compass.

Today, I travel the world to teach this system and how it works. I have set up a method that allows hundreds of thousands of people to earn extra income, on a part-time basis, with the possibility of living completely off marketing.

This is your chance to turn the tide and make the fortune you've dreamed of. I would like to share my experience with those who are willing to listen and take action. I am, according to some, a "legendary marketer", and with Ling-Chih, I am pleased to show you behind the scenes of the top leaders, and help you become YOUR OWN LEGEND too.

PREAMBLE

By Ling-Chih

As a child, Robert loved the carnival. It was one of the few pleasures of his youth, where he could have fun on the roller coaster with friends.

Was it premonitory?

What he didn't know was that his life was going to have its ups and downs like those rides at carnivals.

Let me tell you all about it...

- ***From poverty to wealth, and from wealth to poverty***

Because his start in life was disrupted by family events, he started at the bottom, and reached a status that many will only dream of for the rest of their lives...

Then in turn best salesman, top leader in several Network Marketing companies, high-level trainer, business coach, he and his team generated at the peak of his glory, 400 million turnover in network marketing. Then, he started again from 0 and generated again a huge turnover to achieve success. For example, in the last company, Robert set a personal record, never before beaten, in just 10 days!

And yet, in his early days, nothing predestined him to be so successful...

As you read on, you'll understand how these network marketing stars work.

Robert was born in 1963 in Lille in the north of France. He is the second of three siblings. He comes from a modest family, a mason father and a housewife mother. With addiction problems, an abusive father, and an absent mother, the siblings were left to their own devices from an early age. In the eyes of his father, Robert was the "enfant terrible", the most undisciplined, who deserved to be more supervised. For his father, this meant the belt and the swift.

We're not going to dwell on this painful time, and give voice to Robert.

"When I was 14, we had the misfortune of losing our parents: they were killed in a car accident. Although my childhood was far from happy, it made me determined to find a way out of my life."

"Having become an orphan, my schooling came to an abrupt halt (I must say I wasn't a big fan of studies either). *As a result, my grandparents took charge of the family, which already had 17 children, like all the big families in the north, which was common at the time. There were six people living on the small pension of the grandfather, a former miner. Needless to say, it was hard to live in those conditions. Our menus were always the same: pasta, potatoes, eggs, Jerusalem artichokes... Growing up, I was always on an empty stomach. Sometimes it was difficult to eat enough to satisfy my hunger. My childhood dream was to eat a juicy steak with crispy fries."*

The winter was much harsher than in our time. It often snowed heavily and could easily add up to more than a meter. It wasn't a matter of plows or spreaders, but it was just impossible to get around. As for the weather, remember the famous scene with the excellent Michel Galabru in Welcome to the Sticks (Bienvenue chez les Ch'tis)? *When he informs Kad Merad:* "In summer it's fine, because you're 0, 0-1. But in winter it goes down, it goes down, it goes down: -10, -20. -20, -30. You say: I stay in bed, they give you -40[1]. You see what I'm saying?" *This scene became cult and made 20 million people laugh. It's probably a joke to you, but I swear it was reality and it even happened to have the famous days of -40! Today, it's no more under 40, or even under 10."* Climate change has been there...

However, Robert points out that they were not the only ones to have difficulties: "With the crisis of the 1970s, the closure of spinning companies and mines, everyone found themselves in precarious situations". As a result, this life experience left him little room for fantasy or complaint.

Very quickly, the three children set to work to improve the family economy. At the age of 9, every Sunday, Robert collected potatoes to make pocket money and carried and delivered sacks of potatoes to buildings more than 17 stories high without elevators. His younger sister, whom we will name Line, started working as a home helper at the age of 16. And her brother was studying and working for 3 months in the summer.

---

[1] Those temperatures are in Celsius, -10 °C is 14 °F, -40°C is -40°F.

Life went on like this until Robert was 17. To relieve his grandparents economically, Robert decided to advance the call for compulsory military service. So he left for Compiègne[2], in the army's light aviation. He was a trooper, assigned to the officers' messes. The army taught him how to be a waiter. And he understood, while carrying out tasks that did not interest him much, that his vocation was elsewhere.

When Robert got out of the army, he was 18. He looked for a job in door-to-door sales because it didn't require a degree. He was recruited by La division des Histoires Chrétiennes (Christian Stories Division) de chez Hachette, to become a door-to-door salesman.

- *Meeting with his first mentor*

And then he had his first chance to be trained by a very competent person who taught him his trade. Having received little formal education, he was able to benefit from the training and experience of this experienced mentor. At first, they worked in pairs and little by little,

---

[2] The city of Compiègne is a French city located north of France. The city of Compiègne is located in the department of Oise of the French region Picardie.

step by step, his mentor let him work alone. And he grew out of this experience, as he was elected best salesman and area manager after 5 years.

Then he decided to see the country. A friend told him about a new opportunity to travel and work at the same time. So he was hired at RCI (Resort Condominiums International) to sell leisure apartments on a timeshare basis. It was there that he learned the basics of direct marketing. Thanks to RCI, he travelled in Portugal and all over Europe and became a top salesman there too. Indeed, with his difficult past, he was really motivated to succeed. After a few years, RCI asked him to become a trainer for their employees in Cork, Ireland.

The business has started to turn around for Robert. He started traveling around the world to find clients. He went to Hong Kong, Singapore, the United States. And it was in Thailand that he met his wife and started a family. "It was a beautiful time when I savored the taste of success and I was delighted to be able to get out of poverty," Robert concludes.

• *A new turning point*

Unfortunately, it didn't last long. After a few years, sales became very difficult. The golden age of time-sharing was coming to an end, and it was getting harder and harder to make ends meet. He started working very hard to try to maintain his standard of living. Now he had a family with two children to feed, and he was determined to give them what he never had when he was young. The little paradise he had built for himself gradually became a prison. A prison in which he had to work 60 to 80 hours a week to stay on course. He continued to feed his family, but he no longer had a single minute to devote to them. He worked almost all the time. After a while, what was bound to happen, happened: he had a burn-out. He became seriously ill, three times in a row. First, he had an appendix that got infected, which knocked him down completely for several weeks. Then, as he was very weakened, he got tuberculosis. And finally, the doctors told him he was developing diabetes. During this period, he lost more than forty kilos because of the disease.

"I almost died because of my work. And I can tell you it's VERY scary." That's when a friend decided to help him. She told him about Network Marketing and the Law of Attraction. She explained to him that she was generating very significant income with an activity that didn't look like a job at all. He listened, patiently. He decided to isolate himself in his Bangkok apartment to apply for her advice.

- *Awakening*

"First, *I made my demands to the universe. I prayed for several days. I asked to be able to feed my family without losing my health. Or even my life.*" Then he quit his job, and he started from scratch. He signed up for Network Marketing. He called everyone he knew to tell them about the opportunity. That's when his adventure in Network Marketing began. He gradually developed his network. In France, and internationally. He applied all the things he had learned in his former life to Network Marketing. After a few years, he found himself at the head of a network of several tens of thousands of people. And since then, his network has grown exponentially every day.

Today, he travels the world to teach his methods, which he learned in his former life as a salesman. They enable hundreds of thousands of people every day to earn additional income from Network Marketing. Some are 100% dedicated to it, and live comfortably from it; others generate additional income, alongside their work as salaried employees.

In this book, you will find all the methods Robert used to succeed. Let's get to the core of the matter.

PART ONE:
SUCCESS IS A DECISION AWAY

"Success is a decision. Decide what you're going to do with your life, or someone else will do it for you."

- John Atkinson

STEP #1
THE MINDSET OF THE DOOR-TO-DOOR SALESMAN AND SUCCESSFUL MARKETERS

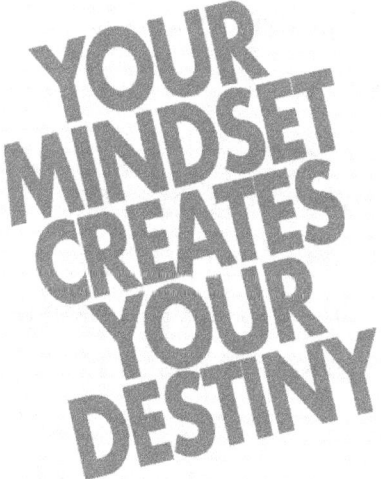

Many people ask me what is the difference between those who are successful and those who are not? My answer is very simple: It's all in your state of mind.

After my first successful sales experience, I understood which character traits were essential to be a top salesman.

Indeed, during my career for 40 years, I have met people who go for all kinds of training, they always think they are missing a technique, a formula, a certificate or a diploma. They believe that they need certain techniques in order to have the legitimacy to succeed.

But that's not true! Succeeding is above all a question of mindset. The proof is that I dropped out of school at 14. My success is therefore not very correlative to my schooling, but is rooted in a mindset, practice and improvement of my actions. A good state of mind is a solid function indispensable to your success. Without it, you build your kingdom on the sand, and sooner or later it is doomed to collapse. It is for this reason that I place the mindset at the beginning of this book, for your business is your projection, and you will start off on the right foot by working on yourself, serving yourself first.

During my career, I've known three types of people: the first ones take action, the second ones observe the others and the last ones don't know what's going on.

What kind of person are you?

- ***The mindset of the top door-to-door salesman***

The mindset of a good salesperson is to wake up in the morning and say to yourself: **I can, I want, I must** and visualize yourself in a successful situation. He puts all the means into action, all the assets on his side and focuses on his vision.

The top salesman lives in the present. He understands that he will be able to change his life and he will strive to achieve his goals. He sees the opportunities in every difficulty. He will really try to put his mind on the opportunity and not on the difficulty.

Of course, everything in life fluctuates and there are always ups and downs. This is called the accordion effect, with the ups and downs. Selling is a very psychological reality and this is built up first and foremost in the salesperson. You have to keep your morale and therefore your positive energy. When the mindset does not follow, we see evil in others. Otherwise, when morale follows, we see good in others. The world reflects perfectly our mindset.

After 40 years of experience, I understood that it is important to develop spiritually, in order to develop an innate sense of observation and respect for others. There is nothing religious about this, because religion is used as a framework. Spirituality is about getting to know ourselves, elevating our soul, broadening our vision of life, being in empathy with those around us. It allows us to get in touch with people, to get to know them better, to better understand their needs, and consequently, to create more personal, effective, and lasting sales experiences.

To become a top seller in your company, you must become rare and different. You must be **action-oriented and** not **reaction-oriented. Act**, so that you don't have to **react** because when you do react, it's already too late. Action is a powerful lever that allows the top seller to get ahead. Becoming a top salesman always creates animosities, jealousies, and frontal or anonymous attacks. So, if you have *haters, on the* positive side, it means you have some success!

Of course, we're not trying to offend others, but a top salesman is in the competition. Of course, not everyone can be pleased with that.

- *Be rare*

What is the difference between the top sellers and the hypersellers? The hyper top businessmen, the billionaires do not create jealousy. On the contrary, **they create envy**. Average salesmen create jealousy because they are in the red oceans of[3] intensive competition. Indeed, there are many more average salesmen than billionaires. Why is that? Because average salespeople have the same targets and the competition is intense.

Staying with average people leads you to stay average. Top sellers always rub shoulders with top sellers in seminars, training, networking..., whereas average sellers don't take any risks and become stars of average sellers, which is, in reality, a glass ceiling that prevents them from going higher and further. The best way to overcome this glass ceiling is none other than to train and surround yourself with partners at the top. If you want to reach the next level, while doing the same thing, believe me, you may spend years without being able to reach your goals. Because if you could do it without changing anything, you would have done it already!

- *Persevere and have faith*

---

[3] According to Wikipedia, the red oceans are the existing activities and represent the known market space. In the red oceans, the boundaries of the activity are known and accepted by the different actors (suppliers, customers, prescribers, etc.). The competition is bloody, hence the term red ocean and the color of the resulting accounts. https://en.wikipedia.org/wiki/Blue_Ocean_Strategy

No one said the road to success is easy. Despite your good intentions and hard work, sometimes you will fail. Some successful entrepreneurs have suffered setbacks and resounding defeats, even bankruptcy, but still managed to get up quickly to make a difference in their fields. Your courage to persist in the face of adversity and your ability to bounce back from temporary disappointment will ensure your success. You must learn to get back on your feet and start over. Your persistence is the measure of your belief in yourself. Remember, if you persevere, nothing can stop you.

- ***Do what you love and don't work a single day for the rest of your life...***

Thomas Huxley once said, "Do what you should do, when you should do it, whether you like it or not". Self-discipline and rigor are the keys to success. The strength of will to force you to pay the price of success: make an extra effort, fight and win the lonely battle against yourself.

From this point of view, we have the impression that the path to success is through the pain. But you can choose not to work anymore, if you do what you like, you will not work a single day of your life! You will live a passionate and exciting life. When some entrepreneurs even though they work 16 hours a day, they are actually talking about a lifestyle driven by passion; they live in "flow", that state of grace when you are completely immersed in your business. The beauty of the "flow" is linked to this maximum state of concentration, full commitment and satisfaction in its accomplishment. It is quite different from forcing yourself to do a job and living it as an obligation.

How do you know if you're good at something? Sometimes you don't even realize it. I'll give you an example from Ling-Chih, my co-author and coaching student. As a member of a non-governmental organization, she is frequently asked to write articles and translate all kinds of texts, from a simple letter to statements to be announced at international summits that she does on a voluntary basis. She does it well and often receives compliments, but has never thought of making a career out of it. It was so easy to do this work for her that she never even thought of getting paid. But even if you don't know any techniques, even if you don't know how to turn your passion into a business, that doesn't stop you from taking small steps and starting to work on your project. We are all creators, and you have to dare to think big before you can experience great things. The mindset is always before the TECHNIQUES!

- ***The Unsuccessful Seller***

He who fails to sell successfully has these traits:

1. Minimum service: unlike salespeople who are passionate about their work, he does the minimum to earn a living and is not very passionate about his work. The reason? Lack of vision. Some people are disillusioned by work and think it is inevitable. "That's how it is in this company", "My boss doesn't listen to anything". Being only an employee and not a decision-maker, they throw in the towel and the same pattern is repeated at home: "my husband always behaves like that", "my mother is super annoying".

    In fact, it's because they too are part of the group they are so critical of. We often possess the traits of the people we criticize and prefer to ignore, it's the mirror effect. In order to avoid this trap, having a clear vision of what you are doing can transform this passive attitude into an active one.

2. Pessimistic: unlike the top seller, he sees difficulties in every opportunity. He automatically looks for obstacles, amplifies them, and takes advantage of them to procrastinate. Basically, he broods and is rather negative.

3. Lack of focus: he is multitasking, instead of focusing on a single project and doing everything possible to complete it, he launches himself into multiple projects simultaneously and scatters. Result: little or no results, no income and he ends up throwing in the towel.

4. Procrastination: the perfectionist often falls into this category. He wants to do so well that he is discouraged by the colossal task. Whereas, if you nibble the elephant, piece by piece, you'll end up swallowing it one day!

• *The mindset of successful marketers*

The fundamental key to success in life is a positive attitude. I say "in life" because the way you do one thing is actually the same as the way you do everything else. There is little difference.

Success is a state of mind. Successful entrepreneurs, Olympic champions, and starred chefs come from a wide variety of backgrounds, but they all have the same mentality: that of a leader.

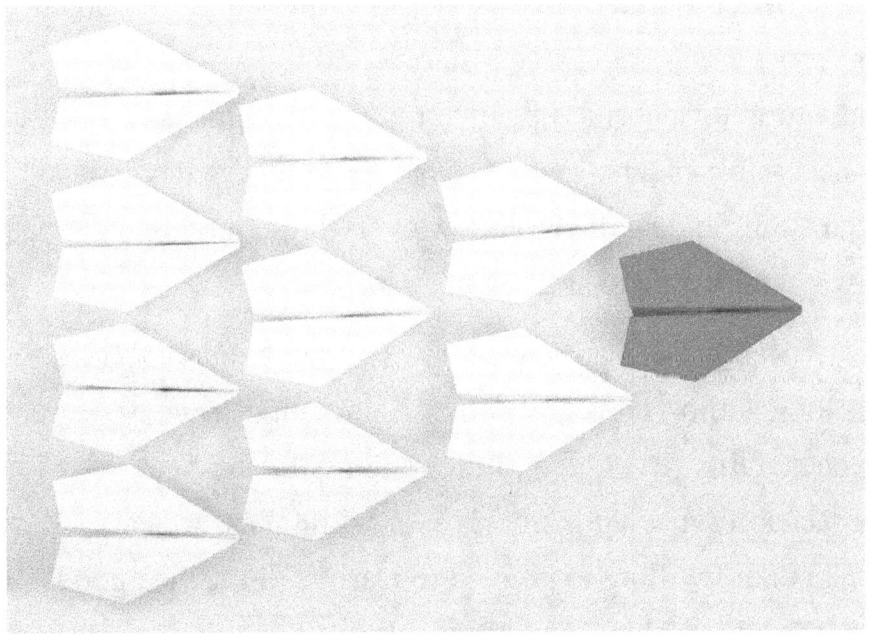

What is a leader? A leader has a vision, he is a leader, a person whose projects and activities are linked to those of the team, in order to satisfy common goals.

As I met my mentor in door-to-door sales, I learned as if to quench my thirst for learning. I soon became very successful and was considered a leader in the field.

In the early 2000s, I became acquainted with Network Marketing. The arrival of the internet changed the way of working considerably and other new professions emerged with the internet fever.

When I joined my first MLM, I immediately wanted to learn. I was eager to get started and train. I needed attention to succeed. I wanted to be with winners, successful leaders. I wrote to my leader every day. I asked questions and wanted to know everything, until one day I was finally able to start on my own.

Kevin Trudeau, a successful entrepreneur and best-selling author, constantly stresses the importance of coachability. Every day, I measure my level of coachability: What is my level of willingness to learn? What am I willing to give up to learn? Do I have a good mindset? Do I have a winning attitude?

You too can examine your attitude. Does it allow you to expand your comfort zone?

- ### *Attitude:*

Your attitude can go in three directions: **forward, neutral, or backward**. Moving forward produces a positive attitude while remaining neutral and/or stepping back produces a negative attitude.

Everyone at some point experiences frustration in life. The question is, how are you going to interpret them? In his cult book "Think and Get Rich," Napoleon Hill gives an inspirational definition of the Great Depression: "The 'Depression' was a blessing in disguise. It reduced the whole world to a new starting point, which gives everyone a new opportunity."[4] It's just a crisis that will allow you to become a stronger leader with a very strong will to succeed.

- ### *Actions:*

---

[4] "Think and Grow Rich!" (The original unedited 1937 text), Napoleon Hill Foundation, 2017.

Another important element in developing a positive attitude is to establish daily actions. There are three key elements in building a professional business in network marketing or life in general: vision, enthusiasm and perseverance.

In order to establish clarity in your action, I invite you to do the following exercise:

1. First, write your **WHY** on a card. Read your **WHY** when you get up in the morning and go to bed at night. The most important force in your life is your **WHY**. You need to internalize your WHY and develop it in your mind.

2. Consult your Mastermind team. Your Mastermind team consists of the first three people you consult every day who will ultimately help you achieve your WHY in life.

3. Talk to three new people a day about your business. These three new people are three new perspectives/three new seeds. "Sowing time and harvesting will not stop". These are two principles that will parallel your success in business and especially in life.

Basically, whatever you plant, you will reap, whether it is positive or negative.

This is an exercise I do regularly with my employees so that the why is firmly anchored in their minds. It contributes to the building of a good foundation necessary for the accomplishment of your business.

A forward-looking attitude will help you build a huge business for yourself and have an incredibly successful life. You can test the result for yourself, starting by reading your WHY card, consulting your Mastermind team daily and talking to three new people a day about your business. If you do this every day, you will see the result after 30 days and this new habit will make a difference.

To be successful, whether in door-to-door sales, in traditional businesses or in Network Marketing, the mentality is always the same. What's special about network marketing is that you work as a team and everyone is an independent entrepreneur. Your success depends largely on the quality of your recruit. Then I will talk to you about how you can find the right people in Network Marketing:

- *The characteristics of right people*

In any business and even more often in Network Marketing, it is said that the most difficult thing was not to develop the network, but to find the 5 partners who want to evolve with it, in order to become confirmed leaders and earn money comfortably. The fact is that most beginners surround themselves with unmotivated people, so, as it is written a little bit above, it is not the fact of recruiting the most difficult thing, it is to recruit the right people:

1. Focus
2. Motivated
3. Persevering

You can do a quick check-up and see what kind of people you work within the team? If you work with partners who are draining your energy, you're going to lose the right people.

STEP #2

KEEP THE MOTIVATIONAL FLAME BURNING NO MATTER WHAT HAPPENS

An entrepreneur is, by definition, someone who takes initiative, initiates projects, and works with his or her vision. It's a path strewn with pitfalls by default and an iron motivation will help you to hold on and bounce back from your professional struggles.

It should be noted that motivation alone will not be enough to accompany you to, and beyond, success. Motivation is the fuel that gives you the energy you need to drive, but if you do nothing, if the engine is inert, having a full tank of fuel doesn't do much good in the end.

In entrepreneurship, you are responsible for ensuring the supply in your vehicle. It's up to you to get the gas at the gas stations or elsewhere. No one is responsible if there is a shortage.

I had a partner who was depressed all the time, who asked his leader to motivate him...His leader can motivate him for 5 minutes, but who is the person who spends more time with that partner? It's himself, 24 hours a day, 7 days a week. If you can't do it, get help from a life coach, a therapist, but don't rely on your professional partner, it's not his role.

I quote below 4 essential pillars of motivation:

Imagine that your life is presented in the form of a temple, supported by 4 main pillars. You have the opportunity to improve your motivational capacity throughout your life, even before using techniques or strategies.

- ***Pillar 1: Gaining peer recognition***

When wartime soldiers give up their lives in battle, why do they do it? Is it because of patriotism, belief in the cause they are fighting for or fear of a court-martial? What is your opinion? Maybe all those things play a role, but extensive research has shown that what really motivates a soldier to fight well is the desire for respect from the person fighting right beside him. This is much more important than medals or other forms of public recognition. It is similar to what motivates salespeople on the floor of a car dealership, students in a classroom, or a team of lawyers trying to win a case.

All football players will tell you that the best reward they wish to receive, is the recognition of other players and to receive the Player of the Year award.

Think of ways to develop peer recognition to improve your motivation and apply it to your life.

- **_Pillar 2: Recognition of respected experts or authorities_**

In my own life, my first Network Marketing mentor helped me, guided me, and became my professional and personal friend. I desperately wanted to earn his respect.

Has there been anyone like that in your life? It is important to realize, that a respected expert does not necessarily have to be someone who is known all over the world. You are the one who sets the qualifications, although very often the people you find impressive will be equally impressive to others.

Once you have met such a person, or even if you just happen to bump into him or her maybe just to read an article about him or her, stop hesitating, approach them politely and introduce yourself. Unless you've come at a particularly difficult time, most successful people are eager to help others and to pass on what they've learned from their experiences.

The key thing about building a relationship with a mentor is that you get close to that person and sometimes you can hear them advising you when they're not really there.

Think about how you can get recognition from a respected expert or authority. You can really stretch this concept to be good parents, local teachers, counselors as well as business people; interpret this in the best way for you.

- *Pillar 3: Family*

While the approval of peers and experts can be important to your career and your life, nothing compares to the influence of your family.

The family is our first social circle, it has a huge impact on our mentality and behavioral patterns. Many of our actions are unconsciously influenced by our parents.

Naturally, we want recognition from our parents and relatives. We want to bring them happiness, well-being, and a comfortable life. Having grown up in a modest family and having lost my parents at the age of 14 gave me a right, a pass to live a life as I want, and as soon as possible. Later, when I became a father, the happiness of my children became one of my priorities and a motivation that touches my heart.

So, think about how your daily life can motivate you and take this into account.

- ***Pillar 4: Share wealth and wisdom for the good of your fellow men***

This pillar is closely linked to No. 3. To illustrate this pillar, I will mention a story I like about Andrew Carnegie, the Scottish immigrant who founded the U.S. Steel Company in the early nineteen hundreds. When Carnegie died, a yellow piece of paper was found in his office on which he had written a note to himself when he was in his twenties. This note illustrated the main purpose of his life. It said, "I'm going to spend the first half of my life accumulating money and I'm going to spend the last half of my life giving it all away."

During his lifetime, Carnegie's fortune was estimated at four hundred and fifty million!

STEP #3
ATTRACT ABUNDANCE INTO YOUR LIFE AND THINK UNLIMITEDLY

- *Let's talk about the Law of Attraction*

Rhonda Byrne's "The Secret", first released as a film in 2006, then published as a book, has become a worldwide bestseller. Apart from that, it has above all popularized the Law of Attraction to thousands of people.

To tell you the truth, I didn't believe it at first. The idea that one could attract things into life by thoughts alone seemed to me to be occult and gibberish.

What made me change my mind was the success and listening to the 14 CDs of Kevin Trudeau, founder of GIN (Global Intelligence Network). I realized that I was unconsciously practicing the Law of Attraction and that I achieved the desired result as a result. My success is exactly the manifestation of this law. Since this realization, I have been a firm believer in it. That is why I recommend that you study it and that you practice it before taking action.

- *You attract what you pay attention to, consciously or unconsciously, whether or not you want to.*

The Law of Attraction is a universal law. It is an obedient law. Understanding this, we want to become more deliberate offerers of the vibrations we emit. This law allows you to get everything you want in life, starting with fulfillment, health, financial freedom, professional accomplishments, harmonious relationships and lasting friendships.

The Law of Attraction works for absolutely everyone. Whether you're conscious or unconscious, the Law of Attraction works for everyone, no matter what your state of mind is. One of the reasons why few people can use the Law of Attraction to get everything they want in their lives is that most people think about what they don't want. It is important to know that you attract what you are focusing on and amplify it by paying attention to it. For example, you want to associate with competent partners, but you look at your current conditions and often worry that you won't be able to do so, or you worry that your staff is struggling to keep up with the company's evolution. Then all these emotions of fear and worry will prevent the moment of achieving your goal, because it is on this fear that you most often focus your attention, and your attention, just like other thoughts, emits an energetic vibration.

- *Using the Law of Attraction to increase our abundance...*

One of the most common questions about the Law of Attraction is to use it to attract more money. Money is abundant energy, so the Law of Attraction can be used to increase the abundance in our lives. To increase the abundant energy, consider this: Law of Attraction depends on the vibrations being emitted.

All energy is vibration. We commonly use vibration to refer to experiences, which have a negative or positive atmosphere. So, when we say we get a good or bad vibe from an experience, we are describing positive vibrations or negative vibrations.

Here is an important concept that is vital to understanding how to use the Law of Attraction: vibrations are generated as a result of the thoughts and words we use. A vibration is simply a mood or feeling. At every moment, we emit a vibration. In the vibratory world, there are only two types of vibrations: positive or negative. The Law of Attraction is a powerful and universal law that simply responds to our vibration, giving us more of the same, whether we want it or not, at every moment, including this moment!

• *Abundance is an emotion*

We have learned so far that all emotions give off vibrations, positive or negative. Abundance is an emotion and that is good news. Why is that good news? All emotions can be reproduced. Abundance is a feeling and that feeling has a corresponding vibration, which we can reproduce. In many cases, people reproduce the feeling of lack, sadness, or despair, simply by the thoughts and words they use. Since we can generate emotions through our words and thoughts, we can learn to reproduce the emotions of abundance more intentionally, using our words and thoughts.

The best news of all is that the Law of Attraction does not know whether we generate a thought by remembering, pretending, creating, visualizing, or dreaming. It simply responds to our vibration at that moment. And we can only contain one vibration at a time! By creating the vibration of abundance more deliberately and more often, we will increase the abundance in our lives.

I suggest that you engage in this process of deliberate duplication of the vibration of abundance, using your thoughts, for the next 7 days. Starting today, here is the exercise that will help you do this.

• *Step 1: Build a list of all sources*

Make a list of all the sources and resources from which money and abundance can come. Most people, when asked, "how could you get more money?" They answered that they could work more, to earn more money. The belief that the ONLY way to increase your abundance is to find a way to earn more money is a limiting belief. There are many other ways that abundance can increase in your life.

Here are 5 sources of abundance. Start with these and create your list of 60 or more sources.

Some ideas for your sources of abundance:
1. Someone invites you to a restaurant.
2. Someone offers you free advice or coaching.
3. You get presents.

4. You benefit from free transport or accommodation.
5. You get clothes for free.

• Step 2: Write down in a daily journal all the sources you receive in abundance

This will greatly help you to notice the abundance in your life. Keeping a journal will show you concrete evidence that abundance exists and is increasing in your life. When you notice abundance, celebrate! By doing so, you magnify the evidence in your life. As you celebrate, know that you are offering the positive vibration of abundance. Think that at every moment, including this moment, the Law of Attraction checks what vibration you are offering, responds to that vibration, and gives you more.

To take action, I recommend that you start with a small step—two minutes a day of deliberate attention to the abundance is better than none at all.

This exercise will make you emit or offer the vibration of abundance more deliberately and more frequently. Have fun with it!

Start doing this exercise over the next 7 days and write down the things you can now start to say to each other. For example: "I am so abundant! I'm attracting proof of abundance every day to succeed!

STEP #4

You deserve the best in the world, keep that in mind

I was suffering from impostor syndrome when I had my first huge success—I thought that I wasn't deserved it and that the success wasn't going to last. Afterwards, I realized that my doubt was because I was a self-taught person. I was happy with the result of my work, but I continued to doubt and to believe that sooner or later, others would find out, that in reality I had nothing and **I was nothing**. I attributed the success of my companies to my luck, hard work, network and timing.

After this realization, I did a work on myself, to remedy the misfortune that had inhabited me during my youth. What good is it if you're not happy with your accomplishment? Being happy is our default feeling, it is a sign that tells us if we are aligned with what we do, what we are and what we desire.

That is why positive self-esteem is very important, if not crucial, to our happiness and well-being as human beings. Having positive self-esteem can make a difference in what we take on in life, in what we will achieve and create. Having a positive self-esteem also allows us to have healthy and joyful relationships with others, to experience true intimacy. We could also say that having a positive self-esteem gives us access to a true spirituality. Low self-esteem, on the other hand, creates the space for us to experience a lot of negativity in life, including depression, anxiety, fear, stress and loneliness. Negative or low self-esteem is also strongly correlated with alcohol and drug addictions. Some even believe that a negative or poor self-image is the cause of such addictions.

Although there seems to be some understanding of the importance of positive self-esteem, the unanswered question has always been how to improve or strengthen a person's self-esteem. Some people believe that a person's self-esteem is based on their success in achieving what they are doing in life or the goals they have set for themselves. As a result, a lot of effort is put into helping others plan effectively for their actions in life. Others believe that our sense of self-esteem is determined by the type of relationships we have, that surrounding ourselves with positive people who will appreciate and recognize us, will positively affect our self-esteem. To this end, training is given to help a person improve their interpersonal skills, their way of communicating and their way of relating to others. While both of these efforts are important, it is not having it or doing it that creates positive self-esteem. Self-esteem is neither given nor obtained from the outside, it is internal to the person.

A very effective way to improve self-esteem is to use positive affirmations. Positive affirmations are very powerful in transforming the negative way a person feels and judges themselves, ultimately influencing their perception and actions in the world and towards others. The fundamental reason why positive affirmations are so effective is that their nature or structure reflects what already exists in our minds. Our identity or who we think we are, our current ways of thinking, are also a series of affirmations, basically composed of simple words or language. Everything we think, all the thoughts we have, are only affirmations. Positive affirmations, when used coherently, begin to alter our widespread internal language model; however negative it may be, our internal discourse or internal dialogue that exists within us. The result of the consistent use of positive affirmations is the transformation of a negative internal language model into a model of a positive nature.

The most effective way to use positive affirmations is to make your voice heard. While a person can have a beneficial outcome by listening to a commercially developed product that uses positive affirmations recorded by another voice, the transformative power of this technology is enhanced or reinforced by the positive messages delivered by one's own voice. By using a person's own voice to transform the inner dialogue, there is less resistance to the transformation process because the voice itself is identical.

It is as if the negative voice or language pattern, which is heard repeatedly in life, is altered or transformed by the coherent exposure and listening to that same voice, but with the structure of positive affirmations. Eventually, the structure will change from a negative structure to one of a positive nature.

PART TWO:
HOW TO DEVELOP, CREATE NEEDS, NEGOTIATE

"I don't have a mentor. Somehow, I am my mentor—I create so I am! It's nice to have a mentor, but it's not an obligation."

- Robert Ingelaere

STEP #5
BRANDING: BUILD YOUR PERSONAL BRAND

- *What is branding?*

You think of McDonald's at the sight of the big yellow arch; you enter a KFC at the sight of that smiling grandpa on a red background; you know that the taxes are writing to you, when you see Marianne's logo on the envelope; it's also when you recognize the unique design style of a fashion designer without seeing his name. In short, branding creates the association between an image and you. Everything is branding: a symbol, a design, a name, a sound, a reputation, an emotion, employees, a tone and much more; that separates one thing from another.

Creating a brand image at the corporate level is common, but today the brand image is becoming equally important at the personal level -- hence the importance of **personal branding**. After all, you might work for a company that collaborates with other companies, but at the end of the day, behind those companies are people working with people and that's what makes business relationships valuable.

- *Why should you build your personal brand?*

When I worked abroad for RCI, we had teams on the streets bringing clients to us and our job was to convince them to go on holiday, every year in 5-star hotels. Now, with network marketing, from crypto-money to paraben-free shampoo, you sell everything, but the goal is to sell yourself - hence the branding.

Building a recognizable personal brand opens up professional opportunities. Creating a vision for your future and implementing it can lead to:

- A better job
- Better contacts and customers for your company
- Industry confidence, credibility and recognition
- And much more...

If you're looking for a better job, you want the potential boss of your ideal company to associate your personal brand with something she needs in her team.

If you're looking to increase a company's sales, you want potential customers to associate your personal brand with a long-term sense of confidence, success and satisfaction.

In today's job market and entrepreneurial landscape, you don't have the right to be just an ordinary face in the crowd. You're unique and you need to let people know that if you want your business to succeed. You need to stand out, be more attractive to your target audience and you can do this by creating a recognizable personal brand.

With my coaching students, one of the aspects to develop is branding. Before selling anything, it is our person who must evoke trust and bring credibility. Branding is the basic before going any further and I am not exaggerating: will you work or buy products with someone who arrives late, poorly dressed or whose clothing does not correspond to the image he tries to convey? The habit doesn't make the monk, but if the monk doesn't wear it, will you be able to recognize him?

I understood the importance of branding when I went on stage—the person who keeps the microphone is always the one who wins the most because you are perceived at that moment as someone credible and authoritative. You are no longer in the position of **follower,** but in the position of **leader.**

- ***Choose what suits you from my advice and take action***

There is a lot of information covering many different steps you can take to create your personal brand.

However, you may not repeat what I write in the book to achieve goals but based on your situation and needs to adjust accordingly.

Everyone's situation and needs are different, so if you notice something that doesn't fit with your vision or goals, rest assured, everything is fine.

I work with online marketers to create branding. You can find marketers who have niche-based mailing lists, with for example 1000 openers. This is a paid service and the price depends on the owner. With a series of mailings prepared in advance – it is best to work with a reputable copywriter - this could bring you fans and then offer them your service or products.

It is also advisable to take professional photos that represent your image. Today you can find very affordable prices. Preferably, you should put the same profile picture in all social networks, to facilitate recognition and show your professionalism.

I had a student whose hair was dry as straw before my coaching. She was used to wearing black or dark clothes. She was already quite reserved and shy, the nature of the black that absorbs light made her old maid and even more serious when she was only in her forties. She rarely wore skirts. To change her look, I recommended that she change her haircut, stand up straight, and wear amplifying bras (yes, men are watching and that's normal. If you have two people with the same skill, who are you going to buy with? The one with a nice shape, or the one who dresses badly?), to change your style from the inside out, and to wear lighter shades that suit h better. After a whole series of transformations, she came back with new professional photos. People started asking her, "Wow, I love your picture, did your coach advise you?" You don't need to spend a lot of money on a makeover, but its effect is immediate, so why not take action?

- *How to create your personal branding vision*

Companies create vision and mission statements. Creating a personal brand begins in the same way by creating a personal vision.

Only you can determine how you want your life to go. You can't control every aspect of your life, but you can create a long-term vision and develop steps to achieve that vision.

The vision of your life should include how you see yourself in 10, 20, and even 50 years. Consider the things in life that would make you happy – is it a family, a beach house, or a fulfilling corporate job?

There are no right or wrong answers, and in this chapter, we will guide you through the steps necessary to create your personal vision.

- *Define your target audience*

Once you have your vision, it's time to determine who your target audience is. Most professionals sell something to someone. If you're looking for a job, you're selling yourself to a potential employer. If you want to start your own business, you sell yourself to potential customers.

But your target audience goes beyond an employer and a customer. You're looking to create a community of people - employers, peers, influencers, etc. - who will be able to share their experiences and learn from each other. - who can all be assets in different ways.

- ***Build your assets online and offline***

There are a number of assets that require special attention when creating your personal brand. You will need to register domain names and websites to control your personal mark when searching. You will need to secure social media accounts to control your personal brand on social networks. And you will need to know how to create these resources so that you can build your global network.

STEP #6
THE EDUCATION OF MILLIONAIRES

- *Employee education*

Conventional education in principle serves to train employees, not leaders. In France, the level of qualification remains closely linked to the level of salary. We hold on to this sheet and there's a good reason for it: a diploma remains the surest way to ensure status and professional mobility. Graduates of the French Grandes Ecoles seem to have earned the precious ticket to employment and an almost guaranteed career plan that so many others desire and envy. Their lives seem to be all mapped out and do not leave a hint of failure. This is a far cry from the American dream, where effort takes precedence over graduation and everyone can try their luck.

It must be said that faced with the high cost of hiring, French companies are cautious and do not want to take risks. They want to take on candidates who are already experienced, instead of leaving a playground for developing employees' potential.

Moreover, the French education system places great emphasis on initial training. If you didn't make the right choice at the beginning or you have changed your mind and want to start a career transition, you have few opportunities in continuing education. Often, you have to go through the small door, an unexpected (or programed, depending on the situation) period of life: for example, a redundancy, or even a burn-out, to have the time, money and opportunity to apply for training at the Pôle Emploi (Job Center) or the Departmental Council. If you have such and such diploma, companies expect you to fit in. If you want to get out of the box, very often companies are so afraid that they will ignore you. After all, except for certain occupations such as catering or sales, where there is a constant shortage of staff, employers are spoilt for choice when it comes to candidates!

Conclusion: if you want to stay employed all your life, it is better to study at the Grandes Ecoles, which will ensure you a comfortable life and meet society's expectations.

I'm not saying it's a bad choice to go into higher education. On the other hand, I do not have any bitterness or lack of an education that I did not receive. I am simply saying that leaders are not conditioned by their environment. They are looking to go outside the box anyway because being a leader is somehow being out of the box. They are aware of the framework and they go beyond what is possible to have an unlimited life.

Without further ado, I will show you how leaders are formed:

• *Leaders are always readers*

Long reserved for a certain elite, teaching is one of its means of keeping the secrets of great knowledge just for them to preserve their superiority in society. By depriving the population of opportunities to learn to read and write, the elite prevents it from being informed and trained. Reading is therefore a primary means of access to information.

Bill Gates wrote a blog post titled "5 amazing books I've read this year" and stated that "Reading is my favorite way to satisfy my curiosity". "Although I get to meet a lot of interesting people and visit fascinating places through my work, I still think books are the best way to explore new topics that interest you."

According to a study by the Centre national du livre (CNL), in 2019, the French read an average of 21 books per year.

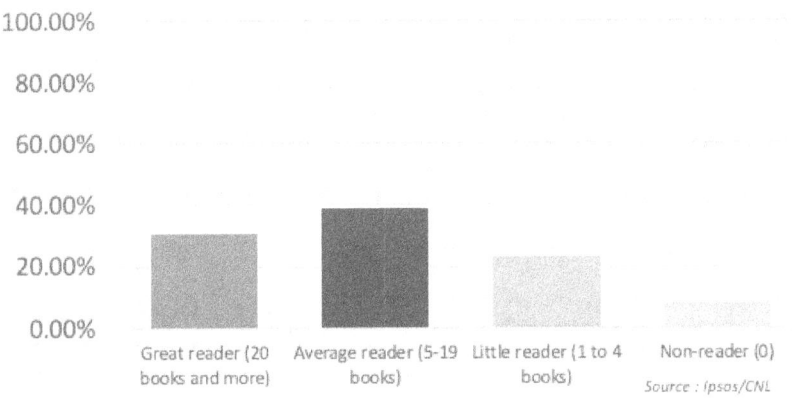

According to Pew research, the American average is 17 books per year. Bill Gates is not in the average; he's totally out of the average: he reads 50 books a year, or about one book a week.

Does that number seem incredible to you? Bill Gates' record is just about average for CEOs: a CEO reads an average of 60 books a year.

If successful entrepreneurs do it, why don't you? It's better to follow in the experts' footsteps, rather than reinventing the wheel.

For my part, I was having difficulty reading with the unexpected cessation of my schooling; I was propelled into the adult world, far from being ready. To remedy this, I worked on myself, reading books on the rich, biographies of successful entrepreneurs, for example, the biography of Marcel Bleustein-Blanchet, the founder of Publicis Groupe. They inspire me in my own endeavors, which means that I quickly get back on track, despite the disappointments and obstacles that all entrepreneurs encounter. They are, in a way, the committee of scientists that I consult when necessary.

If reading is an insurmountable obstacle for you, you can opt for other forms of alternative reading:

1. Television

Some people say that television is the height of stupidity. I was able to overcome my disability and reading difficulties thanks to television, which is for me an important tool to learn what exists in the world. It all depends on your choice. Entertainment channels on nature, music, history, and documentaries can give you a lot of knowledge about our planet.

2. Youtube

Youtube has become very popular in recent years and is the search engine for video. Apart from its entertainment offerings, it is also a platform rich in free training courses. Choose what interests you the most and focus on it, otherwise, you risk spreading yourself too thin.

3. Face-to-face or online training

Thanks to the Internet, the market for info-products is exploding; online training and marketers are gaining impact. Some have become millionaires. For beginners in internet marketing, this territory can seem both promising and frustrating at the same time, due to the lack of reliable information. Another important factor is that 85% or more of online training students drop out of their courses after a few consultations. Lack of support is often cited as one of the reasons for demotivation. In the absence of a system that boosts users to take online training, this mode of learning requires a lot of self-discipline.

Online training is a new continent that coexists with champions and charlatans; and in this 21st century game, price does not necessarily correlate with quality. This is why some people are disgusted with e-learning or are lost in the multitude of choices.

How to choose your online training? I advise you to choose according to the program and the trainer. For beginners who have no knowledge in the field, the best thing is to get coached and to choose coaches by recommendation. Beware, a good coach is not necessarily a question of certificate or experience. In my opinion, these are not criteria that make sense. For me as a network man, the real criteria that count is to ask: *Who do you listen to?* The most important thing is to listen to the right person and a good person is an expert in the field, who has a good network and experiences that match your research. Tell me who you know, I'll tell you who you are!

STEP #7
YOU WANT TO BE THE BOSS? THEN BECOME THE EXPERT IN YOUR FIELD!

I would like to stress the importance of focus. Throughout my career, I have seen entrepreneurs who strive for success, but ultimately succeed in nothing or achieve little. Unfortunately, there are many of them.

Friendly advice: don't try to be like everyone else, refine and focus on your prospect.

One of the easiest ways to attract potential customers to your business is to become an expert in your field. This usually means that your name evokes a direct link to a particular field, which is in fact your trademark. The term Expert carries credibility and prestige. It can open many doors for you and curiously enough, the term Expert is relatively easy to acquire. This simple three-step process can help you position yourself quickly and easily as an expert in your field.

Step 1: Determine your niche

Focus on the things you're really good at. An anecdote: a friend of mine has established himself as an expert in leadership training for wellness client acquisition.

When he told me what he was doing, I asked, "Is there money in it?"

He smiled and replied: "Every city has several, but I am the only wellness leadership expert in my city, frequently quoted in specialized magazines and radio stations as well as invited to speak at their conventions". Find your target and eliminate your competitors.

Step 2: Write about your area of expertise

Once you have determined your niche, start writing articles about your expertise. Every day, tens of thousands of editors, webmasters, and newsletter publishers are relentlessly searching for unique and informative articles. If you can write articles that teach readers about your industry, you will find many places that will quickly publish your article.

Step 3: Talk as often as you can

- **In public**

Once you have become a recognized expert, you will begin to receive requests that lead you to talk more often about your experience.

95% of the population is uncomfortable about speaking in public. So, when you stand up and say what you want to say, the way you want to say it, you're doing what 95% of the population wants to be able to do. When you talk about your expertise, you define yourself as an expert on the subject. You gain credibility instantly.

If you feel nervous when speaking in front of a group, participate in a training or public speaking group. This will be the best investment you'll ever make because the more confident you are in presenting your ideas, the more competent you'll be in front of a group.

Follow these three simple steps and you will become the recognized expert in your specific niche.

- **In private (one-to-one)**

In addition to becoming an inspirational speaker, it is equally important to know how to talk to your prospect either in a small committee or one-on-one. If you are going to talk to a prospect, you need to go through the warm-up stage. Warm-up is an English term that refers to the phase of making information and contact on the spot. It allows you to go further to discover with your prospect his desires, his needs, and his strategies to get there, then convert him into a partner and a friend, with the answers of your prospect. It is his answers that will help you get involved in his future.

In network marketing companies, the warm-up is done on the file. You fill in the file with your prospect and detect his wishes.

Understanding of the following four behaviors:
- liabilities
- aggressive
- assertive
- passive-aggressive

as well as an understanding of the iceberg behavioral pattern, which means that your prospect won't tell you everything, sometimes out of shame or fear of buying, or simply to keep things secret.

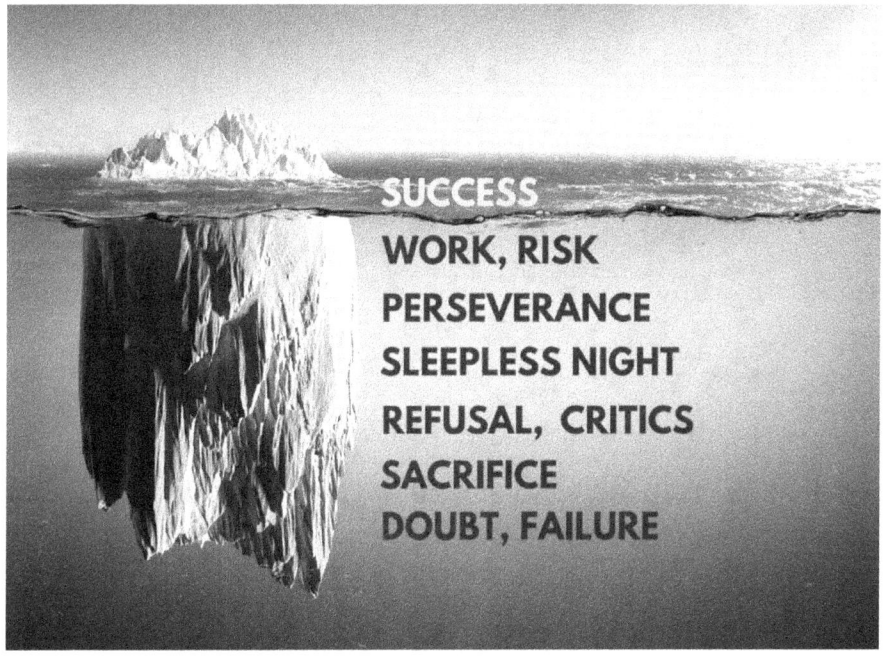

Like an iceberg, our visible behavior represents the tip and is visible to all.

Beneath the surface lies the invisible part of the iceberg, which represents most of ourselves—who we really are—our emotions, our beliefs, our culture, and so on.

The behavior posed by the iceberg asks: "Are you exhibiting behaviors that are consistent with the message you are trying to convey? Or are there unnecessary emotions creeping into your behavior that are distorting the message?"

How to use it?

1. In the beginning, you need to choose a prospect who does not know you.

2. Fill out the questionnaire by asking your prospect questions. Ask for feedback on the areas below:

- Where did the prospect grow up?
- What kind of car do they drive?
- Where do they live?
- What are their hobbies?
- What kind of persons are they?
- What do they do to relax?
- Do they do sports or martial arts?

The objective is to guess the answers, based on what he or she can see, for the familiarization phase.

3. Give yourself the first twenty minutes to write down their answers[5]. Put the prospect's name on the back of a piece of paper.

4. All of these questions have been asked to give you elements and to create a dialogue. You fill in your cartridge with the prospect's answers. Because if you know how to use them well, later on, they will be your weapon to conclude a transaction or a partnership. If this has gone well, the conversation can go on for hours. Otherwise, after the warm-up, the person will take his or her leave.

5. Introduce the concept of the iceberg model, or something similar, before you begin the exercise. Be aware that your prospect is not telling the truth to a salesperson. He will tell a friend. It would, therefore, be wise for you to <u>become his friend and this</u> starts by creating bonds,

---
[5] It takes at least 20 minutes to put your prospect at ease.

conviviality between you. The purpose of this exercise is to bring you together through topics on family, holidays, or work.

No matter how big or small your projects maybe—long term or short term—you have to become the confidant of the person you're talking to, otherwise, it doesn't work. Personally, I have become very close to certain partners, and we have developed a real friendship[6].

Step 4: Give it time

---

[6] On this particular subject, I recommend Dale Carnegie's cult book "How to Make Friends". Published in 1936, this timeless bestseller gives you the basic techniques for influencing others, and that starts with making friends.

Okay, now you're more than ready. You're hot to attack your one, three, five-year plan. In addition to career plans, you set lifestyle goals such as exercise and healthy eating, and you need to implement them in everyday life so that they become entrenched and become habits to be effective.

Most contractors are in a hurry. They never have time to do anything. If that's the case with you, don't worry, you're not alone. But if patience is not your quality, I must warn you that building a business also takes time, planning and, focus; it doesn't happen overnight.

After more than 20 years of activity, a personal assessment prompts me to note that methods have changed since the advent of the internet, new forms of leadership have appeared. Many people are working on their branding.

Twenty years ago, it took years of work to be a recognized leader. Now, to be a leader, it only takes a few months. Our world has changed. There are now voicemails, emails, advertisements, and messaging applications that make "waiting" periods unacceptable and almost obsolete. It's all happening very fast. With information being immediately available, we expect relationships and the achievement of goals to be the same. We know it is unreasonable to expect that. We are led by advertisers to believe that we deserve immediate gratification, just as it is available easily and effortlessly!

When you want to train a partner, you know that it will take time and constant reinforcement. You are ready for this because you want your foal to behave in an acceptable manner. Why then, are you so patient with the partner and so demanding of yourself?

When you plant seeds in the garden, you care for them, water them, hope for sunshine, and feed them. Do you feed yourself?

The best way to move smoothly and effectively towards your goals is to take a sensible approach. Divide your long-term project objective into sub-objectives. Break it down into pieces that are achievable in the short term. Prepare the soil today and plant the seeds tomorrow.

Every action you take and every step you take is satisfying because you know that it contributes to the achievement of your goal. You cannot rush Mother Nature for your garden, and the same is true of your goals.

This process is much more than "flowering where you planted" because when you are a gardener, you choose what to plant and how to grow it. Do the same for yourself and grow yourself beautifully. Your goals will be achieved on time and aligned with your career plan.

• *A little history of marketing and sales*

Marketing and sales are one of the most important elements of a company's survival in the market. While both depend on each other, many people confuse marketing with sales and vice versa, which is a big mistake. Marketing involves designing a product according to market and customer needs, promoting the product through advertising, etc., and setting a competitive price for the product. Marketing is a platform that stimulates sales. On the other hand, the sales process is what you do to successfully sell a product and get a contract. Sales and marketing together are part of the sales process and they are inseparable. The success of a business depends largely on the success of these two essential activities.

Marketing is the backbone of ensuring a sustainable future for the company. While the marketing process encompasses product design, advertising, etc., the sales process is the execution of all efforts that involve direct interaction with the customer, either through face-to-face meetings, cold calling, or networking. But there is always a permanent rivalry between marketing and sales, with one asserting its dominance over the other. Marketers say they have the upper hand because they believe they are the ones who design the products, define the strategy and also develop the tools needed for sales. They say that sales are the result of marketing and should, therefore, follow its instructions. Salespeople may disagree with this view and may be completely opposed to it. They believe that it is the salespeople who actually sell a product and make money for the company.

But many experts believe that marketing should play a pivotal role between the two. A successful marketing campaign facilitates sales. If you're known, it's much easier to convince. Through the creation of a brand or a legend, you become the product reference. You can believe that the salespeople are the leaders, and the sale depends only on them. In reality, if you don't have this marketing support, your talent will be the unique support of your persuasive force. The most important role of the marketing department is to create opportunities for the sales department. Marketing stimulates sales and sales stimulate business success. Marketing is like life support for sales, one that constantly supports the sales department and enables them to successfully deliver the final product. There should not be a race to gain supremacy over another department, but a race to win the market and the customers by working together.

Many companies combine sales and marketing, but in reality, they have different goals. While the sales department is interested in meeting the requirements of what the customer has asked for, the marketing department is actually busy studying what the market demands. The goal of the marketing department is to predict how the market will be formed in the future. They should look at their product to meet the needs of the market for the next few years and be prepared to make design changes to their product accordingly.

It is very important that a company integrates its sales and the department in a well-thought-out way. It is the proper integration of these two important entities that fuels the growth of a company. Salespeople should not be treated simply as cash collectors. Each department has its own role to play which must go hand in hand in the sale of the company's product and must be the most important criterion.

- ***The five secrets that have the most influence on your prospects***

Since you work with human beings, wouldn't it be great to know the five secrets that have the most influence on your clients? What I'm going to share with you will make you the top seller in your niche. I will put them in order of use in the marketing process, but they may overlap or change to suit your situation.

What happens in nature when there's a vacuum? We tend to fill that void, and it is human nature to follow that law.

- *Filling the gap*

When someone does a person a favor or gives something of value for free, this act creates an imbalance in the relationship. It creates a subconscious pressure on the recipient to give something back. This is what is known in marketing to fill the void.

Reciprocity - In marketing, the word "FREE" has the magnetic power to catch the eye of consumers. That's why marketers use it over and over again. Everyone likes free, even if "free" means that there is no obligation or cost, the recipient feels obliged. If something of real value is given to the person, an imbalance is created - a void in nature - that must be filled. Perhaps not immediately, but if that person has obtained great value and usefulness from the gift, there will be a lingering subconscious motivation to return the favor.

You'll find that some people just don't seem to be doing the same thing and they may not have appreciated the full value of your offer. That's why it's so important to ensure that when you offer a free gift with a promotion, your customers are informed of the total value of what they are receiving. A numerical value should be given to the free gift. That is a rate equivalent to the evaluation of the offer. This value makes your "free" offer irresistible, giving an extra reason for your prospect to take action, such as filling out a capture page (which gives you their name, address, and email address), or accepting your product on a 30-day trial period.

Make your customer like you - Have you heard the phrase "if a customer knows, likes, and trusts you, they will buy from you"? Well, you got them to know you through your "free" offer, the next step is to make them like you. The fastest way I know of to get someone to like you is to let them know you love them (reciprocity, again).

Now, not everyone is going to become your fan, but if you take this approach, you have a much better chance of finding customers.

When writing your ads and marketing letters, always write as if it were a personal note to a real, living friend.

Use simple words as if you were talking to your best friend, not fancy jargon. Keep it simple!

Trust - I don't know about you, but when I hear someone say "Trust me" or "Believe me", those are words to banish. It reminds me of a salesman with a hat on and makes me think about not trusting him.

• *How do you trust your prospects?*

So how do you trust your prospects? Play a leadership role with them and tell them what they need to do to act and buy. You need to be or present yourself as an "authority" figure. An expert in your field and the only one they should buy from, as evidenced by the approvals of your other customers, friends, and neighbors.

If your offer is made in a letter, include some mention of others, mention articles written about you, books, articles, newsletters you have written, etc. It's common that most people don't want to make a decision, and it's best that you give them a plan of action for saying "yes".

Rarity - It is a mode of persuasion that really motivates prospects to act, you need to create and manage this to your advantage in every offer you make.

People want things that solve their problems or make them feel good about themselves and that is of good quality. They want it even more - if the quantity is limited in some way. (Remember the law of supply and demand?) If demand for a product is high and supply is low, the price will be easily accepted.

Even if you create the "perception" that there is a limited quantity available, a limited timeframe for availability, or whatever you plan to use, you will find this to be a catalyst for your client's action, more commonly referred to as "creating urgency".

Of course, it goes without saying that you always include some kind of guarantee in your offers. I always like the "no questions asked" type of guarantee for 30 days. With this, you insist on your credibility (trust) by saying that you will be there for a certain period of time. I've found that most of the time, the warranty policy you offer has very few takers, and if there are - you don't want to keep a dissatisfied customer anyway. The refund is immediate and the customer will be removed from the lists.

Be sure to include these five tips in all your offers:

1. ads
2. sales letters
3. presentations
4. rare
5. emergency

You will see spectacular results and an increase in your activity.

STEP #8
THE ART OF PERSUASION

Whether it is for a sale or a coaching session, it is never too much to stress the importance of a well-structured speech as an essential step to an effective presentation. Not to mention the non-verbal part that influences up to 80% of the audience's opinion of the speaker.

When I was a door-to-door salesman, my mentor taught me the importance of sales pitches. After all, why would an average prospect open the door to me without knowing me? How do you go knocking on people's doors to get them to open the door for you? And how do you get people to get a good first impression of you? I will suggest some exercises on this subject later.

- *First impressions*

Convincing people of the importance of first impressions. The fact is that people get an idea of you from what you say and what you do. There are two parts to this: 1. you need to know how you present yourself; 2. you can put on a character to create a strong first impression, even if you are nervous.

Discuss how first impressions are formed based on behavior alone.

The completion time is 20 minutes (warm-up / reheating). The longer it takes, the more your prospect becomes your friend.

Task

1. You will have to choose a partner you don't know.

2. Write your comments on the areas below, without showing them to your partner:

   1. Where their partner grew up
   2. What kind of car do they drive?
   3. Where they live
   4. What are their hobbies
   5. What kind of person are they?
   6. What do they do to relax?

The goal is to guess the answers, based on what you can see.

3. You will have five minutes to write your answers. You must put your partner's name on a piece of paper and give it to your coach to keep safe.

Learning objectives:
- How to create credibility in your business
- Recognize the essential do's and don'ts for perfect presentations
- Keeping the audience's attention throughout the presentation
- How to offer powerful beginnings and endings
- How to structure your presentation to deliver your key messages
- How to recognize and maximize the strengths of your presentation
- How to hide visible signs of nervousness
- How to write impromptu presentations
- How to maximize voice projection to create impact
- How to use powerful body language
- How to deal with difficult audience issues

- How to use audio and visual aids to support your message

After my experience in door-to-door sales, I understood that each person has his own argument, so I developed mine based on the product and put my personality into it.

In the same way, I recommend that you appropriate these techniques and adapt them to your personality, so that your argument is well integrated, fluid and natural.

STEP #9
DEVELOP YOUR SUPER BRAIN

Becoming a successful entrepreneur requires a certain amount of brain capacity, for example, memory: How do you remember the names of your clients or people you meet for the first time, or after a few months? Since everyone's name is the most beautiful melody that resonates in his ears, the more you sing, the more you charm him. Other examples: remembering the content of a training course or a seminar, remembering the date of birth of your best customer? The importance of memory is without a doubt.

My advice to keep your memory in good shape

Leaving school at the age of 14 may have been complicated at the time, but it was ultimately a blessing in disguise so that one could learn without delay and be propelled into the school of life.

In this school of societal life, it is recommended to work on your brain, which is similar to bodybuilding: the more you work on your muscle, the firmer and more toned it will be. It's the same for the brain. Keeping memory in good condition is a vital part of brain function. From time to time, our actions depend heavily on the many pieces of information we retrieve from our memory bank. This information can be short-term (such as specific tasks we have to perform) or long-term (such as being able to drive a car or repeat an instruction from a book). Although long-term memory can come spontaneously, without too much effort, when the need arises, short-term memory requires us to recall information from the accumulation of things stored in our memory. This is why you need to keep your memory in good shape to be effective in your daily tasks:

- **Focus on the information you need to store in your memory bank.** Even with distractions around you, stay focused on the subject. The more focused you are on the information, the better chance you have of keeping it in your memory.

- Use the most ideal sense or senses when collecting information. This is what we call acuity, in the detection of our environment. Be aware of the color or detail of an image, or the particular sound or smell of the element involved. All our body senses are listening, to gather information according to the circumstances. While our sense of sight can be used most to gather information, our senses of hearing, smell, taste, and touch are equally important and useful for remembering things, situations, and information about something or someone.

- If you are not sure that the information you are going to remember will actually be retained by your brain, it would be better to write it down. This could be effective, especially for gathering very long and tedious information, such as conference notes or personal interviews. Just make sure you don't forget that you have a note on hand; and of course, keep it in a safe place.

- **Maintain a balanced diet.** A well-proportioned diet promotes a conditioned memory. Fatty and sugary foods can confuse memory. If you cannot completely eliminate a poor diet, gradually reduce your intake of these memory-inhibiting foods. This will gradually lessen the effect of withdrawal symptoms and you will adapt to the new lifestyle you are creating. This will be good for your memory and we can say that you are on the verge of living a healthy life. Drinking lots of water has many benefits for your overall health and memory is no exception.

- **Get enough rest and sleep and sleep according to your schedule**. Getting enough sleep does not mean laziness, quite the contrary. We are not a machine, and sleep helps our bodies to function properly. So, don't feel guilty about rest or sleep as long as it's not excessive. Dr. Michael Breus explains in his book "*When? - Make your chronobiological revolution and fully realize your life*" that each one of us has unique chronobiology, and it would be advisable to find your chronotype. You need it badly to keep you revitalized from the tedious demands of work.

- **Take some time to relax.** Breathe deeply on a regular basis and under stress. Keep your thoughts organized before acting on them. Move away from stress and anxiety. It may not be possible to completely eliminate stress because it is part of our generation, but try to reduce it as much as possible. Stress can bring your memory to its ineffective level. Avoid the habit of telling yourself that you might forget things, as you are more likely to do so. This simply reinforces your anxiety level to its panic mode.

- **Stay positive, creative, and energetic.** Your memory should be in a circle of things. Objects of different shapes, sizes, and colors can motivate your creativity. This is a positive way to discover your environment in all its variations and diversity. Avoid shutting yourself in the four walls of your room, as if you were a prisoner. The only time you need to be locked in is when you need to rest or sleep. Don't be a couch potato. There is a very exciting world out there waiting for you to improve your memory.

The best time to improve your memory is between infancy and adolescence. As you get older, your memory begins to fail. But a strong memory that we can develop in the early years of our lives will certainly help us to be good thinkers. This can be done by continually exercising our memory through reading and other cognitive activities, such as the habit of solving crosswords. The more you do, the better your memory retention.

From a health perspective, high blood pressure can lead to strokes and heart disease. It also leads to poor memory retention. Memory function decreases when blood pressure is high. Researchers have found that people with normal blood pressure, especially in their forties, have higher cognitive function. Concentration, decision-making, and memory functions are impaired by high blood pressure. What is healthy for the body is also healthy for memory.

STEP #10
KNOWING WHAT YOU REALLY WANT AND SETTING GOALS

For many people, success is a fairy tale and they don't even think they have access to it. In reality, success is fast approaching and sometimes already exists as a hidden treasure. I am referring to the skills you already have, friends and family who will help you, and the accomplishments you have already made.

Success can easily be compared to a treasure locked in a bottle. You see it, you're close and yet it remains elusive. For many of us, it's all about finding a way to open the bottle and then following a specific path. That path is full of pitfalls and traps, so it's wise to broaden your vision by learning as you go.

I've come across a lot of people in my life. Sometimes I meet people who want to succeed but don't know what they want and have difficulty making decisions. The reasons are very varied. I can cite a classic case: Franck (pseudo) is a salesman in a luxury boutique and has been working there for years. He is interested in my coaching because he wants to change his life, but he doesn't know what to do or what he wants.

Very often, people unconsciously follow the values of society, of parents, of other people, without really looking for what they want. This path may guarantee a comfortable life, but it does not necessarily correspond to the real will of the person. Conventional education reinforces this formatting through the transmission of conforming values.

I am not saying that it is bad to follow a school curriculum like Mr. and Mrs. Everyman, I would like people to be aware of their choices and their actions because if you do not do so, your deep desire will end up being expressed in one way or another. For years, the person can lead a peaceful existence, receive compliments from everyone, until the day the shell starts to crack, a burn-out that forces you to stop immediately. So, before you get to that point, and you wake up in the night and wonder what you are doing there, I advise you to do some work on yourself and get help.

If, on the contrary, you recognize these hidden treasures, gather them together, and keep your final goal in mind and keep this yearning alive, then you are on the road to success. Let's see how to progress every day, to live a quality life and help everyone around you in the process.

Write down all your goals on a piece of paper and keep them in a prominent place that you can easily access on a daily basis. This could be on a piece of paper in your pocket, on your desk, in a notebook, in your diary or on your smartphone. Wherever you put this information, it should be a place where you will see it every day.

Separate realistic goals from high goals, but keep the goals high. In addition, separate short-term goals from long-term goals and develop estimated timeframes for measured results. Only share with someone who has the same goals as you do. If you have at least one close friend, spouse or family member who shares the same dream, you are in a very strong position.

However, you don't have to be a "politician" to be successful if you learn to focus on your goals every day.

We now need to review a few questions, which will also help you design your roadmap to success.

- ***Will your goals hurt anyone? Will you have to step on someone to get what you want?***

If you answered yes to any of these questions, you need to redefine your goal(s) so that you can achieve them without hurting them. If this is not possible, start this goal and continue. Your goal(s) should help people and be morally sound.

- ***Do you have a real passion for your goals?***

This is also important because if your goal is to "flip burgers" for a living, you haven't yet found the real why. I haven't yet met the person, who has a real passion for flipping hamburgers. Please don't get me wrong, some people are very good at it, but I know many short-term cooks who would like to do something other than "work" on a hot stove.

What you choose, must be something you like to do and the money will follow. There are so many people who create an occupation based solely on money and then learn to regret it.

In fact, if you do what you like, you will attract followers and you will have fans. Money is an energy that vibrates with the emotion of abundance - joy, passion, enthusiasm, that's why if you work with a burning desire, you are more likely to attract fortune.

STEP #11
CLOSING OR HOW TO GET A SALE

In any business, whether it's a traditional or network marketing company, closing your prospects is a crucial step in moving your business forward. You may be the best at prospecting, inviting, and presenting your business, but you still need to close them. Closing is all about making a proposal and especially the step where you close a sale and then collect the money. The viability of your business depends on it. That's why this last step can make or break your business.

The first thing you sell is the salesperson/contractor/marketer, in this case, you. In order to make a sale, it is essential that your prospect **perceives** more value in you and your company than in your competitors. This **perceived value** must also **correspond to** his needs. If you or your offer is no different in the eyes of the customer, all that remains is the price as a variable element. Is your offer adapted to the customer's needs?

Esther and Jerry Hicks, the messengers of Abraham (a spiritual entity made up of instructors who are not part of our physical reality), wrote a best-seller entitled "Ask and you shall receive". The closing is actually very simple: **just ask. If it is accepted, then the deal is done**! It's as simple as that.

In Network Marketing, achieving an income equivalent to a full-time job or more by doing what you love requires people to join your team and customers to buy products. Professionals go through a process before moving on to closing.

Before you leave any doubt, here's the good news: you can acquire the skills you need to close more leads. The more you do, the better you can do it.

- *Identify the decision-maker*

Whatever sector you are in, identifying the decision maker is crucial for an efficient closing. Very often, decision-makers send someone else to the front to take as much information about your company as possible. If this is the case, make sure you put yourself in the decision-maker's shoes so that you can personalize your sales pitch, based on that person's interests, even if he or she is not there.

Of course, the best scenario is to sit down with the decision-maker. Do everything you can to set up a meeting with that person.

- **Straight to the goal**

Every transaction has a logical order, a purpose. You need to be clear about why you want to meet your prospect, what are your desire and your goal? Today, people have no time to waste, and it is always better to be frank, direct, and honest with your future client. So, don't beat around the bush, and don't venture onto the slippery slope of lies. In business, lying is never necessary, rarely useful, always dangerous (negative comments always spread faster and longer than positive ones). A customer can sense if you are authentic during the sales process. In other words, it is important to let the customer know that you are interested in him and not just in the deal. Over-calculated behavior can discourage people. However, remember that there is nothing wrong with being well prepared. It is normal to appear as if you are ready to answer all the questions you will be asked. Quite simply, act in the best interests of the client, for a win/win result.

To sell is to seduce, to please, to give desire!

- ***Create a sense of urgency and connection with your prospect***

In order to achieve an objective, it is necessary to determine a duration in time, a deadline. Set a deadline for the transaction, to help motivate the client to commit. Whether it's a rebate or something free, make them feel they have the upper hand. This doesn't mean rushing the customer; it just means trying to give them a little extra reason why your product or service is the right choice for them and the right choice right now. Rushing works as long as you know the reason and purpose of the customer's purchase.

It's up to you to position yourself, to lead the dance to set a deadline, otherwise, you risk getting swept away and coming home empty-handed.

Each time you give information or the person you're talking to shares his feelings, try to find out what he thinks: **"What do you think?"** That word is your pass into the prospect's heart. **Without "what do you think?" you're a thief and/or rapist. With "what do you think?", you're attractive without being seductive.** With this process, your interlocutor is more likely to open up to you, and if he opens up to you, he opens up more easily to your proposition.

This opening leads to the discovery of the prospect's need, conscious, or unconscious. Whatever the case, it is up to you to make it visible and to show that irrefutable evidence—in most cases, his own words—to your prospect, so that he understands that his situation will improve and that you are the right person to provide a solution to relieve his pain and solve his problem.

- ***Overcome objections***

Preparing the sales presentation to process and overcome potential objections can speed up any transaction. If something surprises you, you may need to take some time to find a solution. By having an overview of anticipated problems and thoughtful risk analysis, you can reduce resistance.

I strongly recommend that you sit down with your entire sales team and ask each person to formulate any objections they might expect. Give them your sales pitch and see if there are any objections that you and your team might have missed.

- *Know your competitors*

Competition between companies is fierce. Knowing where you are more competitive than your competitors can lead to this rapid closure. Once again, it's all about preparation. Do your research and make sure you write down something you do that your competitors don't do. This is often the biggest selling point, so don't ignore it.

There are three types of preparation:

    A. Personal Preparation

Prepare yourself physically and psychologically. Dress professionally -- dress *for success*!

B. Preparation for sale

Equip yourself with all the prospecting tools, prospectus, video, price list, membership form, order form...and a good operational computer.

C. Prospect preparation

Its basic information, its needs, its objective, its dream, its concern...

- ***Always prefer face-to-face meetings***

Although we are in the age of hyperconnection, always prefer face-to-face closing; don't do it on the phone, or on Messenger, WhatsApp or WeChat. Remember: 70% of communication is non-verbal: how can you feel your client's emotions and transmit your energy and passion? And it's much harder to turn someone away in front of you than online. You can't "block" him either, at least not right away!

Being competent at closing is undoubtedly one of the most important techniques a seller can master. Learn this technique from a mentor or an experienced salesperson, practice and take action, you too can become an ace in sales.

Do like an ace!

Checklist in 5 minutes on top sellers/unsuccessful sellers

To become an ace in sales, you need to know what top salespeople do and gauge your level.

	Top sellers	Average sellers	Unsuccessful sellers
Mindset	He has the faith to become a top seller before taking action	Thinking "I'll try it."	Don't think he's going to make it
Value	He thinks that selling is a profession that allows him to make a fortune	He's taking the sale for an opportunity that allows him to have an additional income	He's taking the sale for a business that allows him to make up his income
Number of visits to the customer's premises	5-10/day	1-2/day	0

Team Communication	4-5 times/day	2-3 times/day	0-1 times/day
External Communication	Being comfortable with objections and know how to answer	Lack of fluidity when dealing with questions	Cannot answer questions of customers
Objective	Take action in a planned manner according to plan	Lack of precision in objectives	No objective
Training	Spontaneous to learn communication, follow-up and customer service. Regularly follow professional training	Using the wrong methods. Learn only at the request of your leader	Doesn't learn anything
Attitude	Focus, attention, action	Take action only when the opportunity arises comes along	Don't you dare to take action and always makes excuses

STEP #12
ORGANIZATION OF TIME

- **Strategies to maximize time**

There is no denying the saying: "Time is money".

You never seem to have enough time. Even if you were given 30 hours a day, you still couldn't get enough. Somehow, some things will happen and you'll end up wanting more time. Time is a precious commodity. Once it's gone, it's irretrievable.

The fact is, when you're busy, time flies. But when you're not, time seems to have stopped. This is true when you are killing time, because there is nothing else to do under the circumstances.

How do you maximize the use of your time? It would be helpful if you took the time to consider the following strategies:

- ***Check your schedule at the beginning of the day. Review it in its entirety.***

You may notice that some parts of your day can be hectic, while others may not be too frenetic. Distribute your activities evenly throughout the day.

Keep notebooks handy so you can keep track of your schedule. It also helps you remember your tasks and commitments. Notepads and planning notebooks help you avoid duplication of effort. If there is an overlap, determine which one has priority.

After you've divided up your schedule for the day and still feel overwhelmed by the number of tasks you have to do, you may want to forget some of them. Reschedule other tasks for another day.

What you're actually doing is a lot like cleaning out a closet. When your wardrobe is in order, you avoid getting a headache from falling objects when you open the door. Also, if it's convenient for you, you'll probably find some space available.

- *Ask for a new planning in advance*

This is especially true when another person is involved. Showing courtesy in doing so is moving forward.

It gives the person time to adjust to the new schedule. Who knows? You may be doing the other parties a favor. They may be in the same situation as you and they won't know unless you tell them.

- ### *The Pomodoro technique*

Pomodoro is a time management technique developed by Francesco Cirillo in the late 1980s. The name Pomodoro comes from the tomato-shaped kitchen timer that Francesco Cirillo used with students. The technique uses a timer to divide work into intervals, traditionally 25 minutes, separated by short 5-minute breaks.

The Pomodoro Method suggests that you work for 25 minutes, devoting yourself fully to the task, then take a five-minute break. You can observe how much time you spend on a task, and see if you can divide it into smaller portions for example. The idea is to find a balance between concentration and relaxation, consume without moderation.

- ***Be creative***

Time is an element where simple creativity can be put into practice. For example, you have to do the laundry, but at the same time you also have to hurry to do your shopping. Maybe what you can do is to wear out your washing machine to do the laundry, while you go out to the grocery store. Manage your time at the grocery store and at home, just at laundry time.

You can even cook at the same time using a slow cooker. It cooks the food by itself. You can even pick up the kids from school after shopping. Four are weary in one. All it takes is planning and a little creativity.

- ***When you have to perform a task for the first time, it is natural for errors to occur.***

However, a first task should not be a mistake. If there is no weary indication of how things should be done, take the time to plan before taking action. This saves time, energy, and money.

- ***Visualize the possible outcome of your goal. Look for alternatives.***

Choose the best of two or more alternatives. If there is only one option, do the same. Some may seem difficult when you think about them, but not necessarily when they are implemented. The same is true the other way around.

Time is something he's tired of optimizing. You become wise when you choose to maximize.

PART THREE:
REJOICE IN WHAT SALES AND MARKETING CAN BRING TO EVERYONE - IT'S ALSO A LIFESTYLE!

"The best way to predict the future is to create it."

- Peter Druck

STEP #13
NETWORK MARKETING: A TURNKEY BUSINESS

- *Why start a Network Marketing business?*

To get rich, it's everyone's dream. Some people want to make money by owning their own business. All successful entrepreneurs have the self-discipline to start their own business. Most of us have heard the adage "it takes money to make money". Basically, that means you have to put money into your business if you want to make money.

A Network Marketing company allows you to work part-time. It allows you to generate a generous residual income. And it makes you the owner of a small business. Network Marketing has already created many millionaires. They are living proof of how hard work is: continuous prospecting, motivation, and training of others pay off.

If you ever decide to join one, you should take note that you are embarking on something that is modeled on what you are capable of. It will be an assurance that you are capable of anything to succeed.

In practice, about 24% of small business start-ups fail within two years. Indeed, the life of your business depends on you during its first years. If you have to rely on the business, it will probably fail. The first few years of a business are rarely profitable because you are reinvesting your money in it.

Most of us spend money on entertainment, whether it's eating in good restaurants, movies, cars, bikes, games, big toys, etc. ... If you want your business to grow, you have to feed it. You have to spend money to make money, even if it is a small amount, it will increase again. To win, you have to invest, like if you want to win the lottery, you have to buy a ticket first!

All successful entrepreneurs spend a certain amount of money each month on their business. Of course, you say they make money, so they have to spend it. But in reality, you start investing a larger percentage of your profits, and then you'll do it later, as your business grows. Most people who start a business offline usually invest a lot of capital before they see any money come in. You have to continually invest your money.

This is where online business is unique. You can start with very little capital and invest as you learn. You still need to invest money and time if your goal is to grow. You have to spend wisely, however, where you will see results. You need to read and research before you spend. There are many ways to spend your money if you are new and not paying attention. There are also many ways to receive valuable information online for free. One way is to read free articles written by successful people.

Also, if you are in an MLM or affiliate program, you should have an online leader. He will help you with good advice because it is in his interest that you succeed!

For my part, I entered network marketing in 1996, thanks to the recommendation of a friend. Since then, I've worked in several MLM companies and I've succeeded in the third one thanks to my mentor.

The reason I'm telling you this is that you've probably heard that only a small portion (5%) of all home-based contractors are successful? Do an online google search and you'll see what I mean.

I also reveal my criteria on MLM: I chose network marketing companies based on leaders, years of creation and momentum. It takes at least 6 years of existence for an MLM company to show validity and solidity. You don't want to join an MLM and work hard just to see it crumble after a few years!

I will show you the key to success for home-based entrepreneurs; you will discover what makes an entrepreneur successful in the home-based business sector.

Here are 5 tips for home-based contractors:

- ***The key to your motivation and success***

What distinguishes people who succeed in the lot? Is it money, luck, and/or talent? No, it's a simple little fact - motivation.

Successful entrepreneurs all share a common trait: they are motivated. Serious entrepreneurs have "programmed" their minds to succeed, no matter what. They are 100% focused on their home-based business and don't let anyone stop their plans to achieve what they want. They are determined.

Successful entrepreneurs know what they want and have the desire to succeed. If you're not sure what you want when it comes to your home-based business, think again and rethink your plans, what you want to achieve, a fast and profitable business over the long term.

Of course, motivation is not simple at all. That's why there's a multi-billion-dollar industry focused on personal development books, online training, seminars, internships, and coaches.

There is only one problem with the use of these methods. As far as motivation is concerned, one size does not fit all. One of the things that makes human beings so infinitely fascinating is that we are all different. This is the main reason why our species is so successful. It also means that we each have different interests, goals and motivation.

So, before you can start taking any of the thousands of motivational programs available, you must first determine which motivational group you belong to.

After these years of working with professional partners, I summarize them in four basic categories of motivation:

1. The pessimist
2. The competitor
3. The minimalist
4. The exhibitionist

1. The pessimist

You certainly know a pessimist around you. One of my leaders is working with a partner who is constantly brooding. Every time he gets the slightest bit of bad news, he immediately jumps into a bottomless pit and plunges into sadness. No matter how big or small the problem is, he often reacts as if it is the end of the world. If his internet box is momentarily out of order, he immediately assumes that the bill has not been paid, the bank account has been closed, and it's immediately a disaster.

I drew the line but my leader took a long time to manage this partner. At first, he thought it was panicky and he was trying to protect him from the small, and even big, worries of life. Later, my leader understood that this is actually how he was motivated.

When faced with challenges, big or small, he goes through them in a familiar cycle. First, he describes the worst-case scenario, then he describes his options for action, and then he takes action. And when he acts, move away because he moves very quickly and successfully. Challenge met; problem solved. It drives my leader crazy, but it works for him!

2. The competitor

The brother of a leader, Pierre, feeds on the competition. Whether he plays sports or works in sales, he is always more successful if he has competition. If his motivation is an indicator, he can easily pull himself together by quickly comparing his progress towards a particular goal against others. He likes to keep the score and this keeps him motivated. He wants to win whatever competition is at hand.

Be convinced by this method! In almost every measure, Pierre has had enormous success and has managed to grow from a contract employee barely able to afford his two-bedroom apartment to a top-level sales manager with a six-figure salary plus bonuses to give him more incentive.

3. The minimalist

Minimalists have a short attention span and tend to for **Attention Deficit Disorder**. They need short-term goals that are immediately visible and can be achieved in a short time. They can go the distance as long as it is divided into small projects. Each small victory will motivate them to reach the goal, but they need these small successes to keep them motivated.

4. The exhibitionist

Nothing to do with a pervert, the exhibitionist is someone who struggles with invisible objectives. Like the minimalist, it is recommended to divide large projects into bite sized pieces so that they are not so overwhelming. Divide the stack of work into several smaller stacks, so that you can feel progress more easily and quickly.

But it's not enough to just get the task done - you need a to-do list that you can check off as you go along, then cross them off one after the other when you've done them. An exhibitionist must be able to point to a visible success for the day, whether it's a shiny kitchen, a pile of filed papers, or a pile of finished handwritten pages.

Which category do you belong to? Once you know a lot about yourself, you will be better able to find the motivation technique that suits you best.

- ***Choose a good Network Marketing company***

Here are some tips you may want to consider before choosing one:

1. **A company that you like and are interested in.**

One of the best ways to find out, if this is the type of business and plan you want to promote, is to see if you are interested in buying the product yourself. If so, chances are many other people are also interested in the same program and products.

2. **Look for a high-quality company.** For example, look for one that is associated with many experts in that particular sector. This way, you are assured of the quality of the program you will be joining.

3. **Join those who offer real and viable products.** How do I find out? Do some initial research. If possible, find some of the members and customers to give you a testimonial on the credibility of the program.

4. **The product that responds to a growing target market.** This will ensure that there will be more and continuing demand for your references. Find out more. There are forums and discussions you can participate in to get reliable, quality feedback.

5. **A business with a compensation plan that pays a residual income and a payout of 40% or more would be an excellent choice.** 40% sounds like a lot, except that everything is included, including marketing and commission, so in reality MLMs only pay 27-28% commission. Some companies offer this type of payment. Look for one. Save your time by selecting companies that substantially reward your efforts.

6. Be aware of the minimum quotas you have to meet or the sales target that is too difficult to achieve. Some Network Marketing companies impose preconditions before you can earn your commissions. Just make sure you can meet their requirements by asking yourself the right questions.

7. Select the one with the many tools and resources that can help you grow your business in the shortest possible time. Choose the affiliate program(s) that have these capabilities. Make sure they have many useful tools that you can use.

8. Check whether the program has a proven system that can allow you to verify your networks and your remuneration. Also, check if they have it available online so you can check at any time and from anywhere.

9. Choose a program that offers strong incentives for members to renew their membership each time. A Network Marketing company that provides ongoing support and upgrades for its products tends to retain members. These features can help your networks grow.

10. **Be aware of the things that members are not satisfied with a business.** Like those mentioned above, you can check on the discussion forums. If you know someone in the same program, it is important to ask if there are many drawbacks.

Have in-depth and intensive knowledge of a Network Marketing company you will be promoting.

Knowing the type of program you are embarking on will allow you to anticipate and prevent any future problems you may encounter.

- *Establish a start-up plan*

Savvy entrepreneurs know that it takes time to create and develop a profitable home-based business. They plan to succeed. They have a start-up plan that could fail, but they always persevere and start over with a better plan.

Serious entrepreneurs know that it takes time and discipline to build a strong, solid home-based business that generates continuous income for many years.

• *Do an initial search*

Smart and serious entrepreneurs know the importance of market research. They know that to be successful in their home-based business, they need to study their target market (their potential customers) and study their competitors.

Study your target market and study your competitors to obtain a profitable home-based business in the long term.

Know what your customers want and give it to them. Watch your competitors, study their offers, and make sure you offer something better than they do.

• *Build a winning marketing strategy*

Study every successful entrepreneur in your marketing field and you'll notice how they market online/offline.

Each has its own "unique" marketing strategy but uses the same basic principles.

Use the main proven marketing concepts, try to improve them, and adapt them to your own situation. Make them work for your home-based business. Make your offer better and more unique than your competitors, if you want to win in this business!

- ***Invest your time and money***

Smart entrepreneurs know that the key is to work smart and strategic, but not difficult. If you don't have the skills to develop a new marketing tactic for your home-based business, why not hire a coach who knows the business?

If you have the funds, why not invest in someone who can help you grow your home-based business and give you something to work with?

What is more valuable to you, your time or your money?

A serious entrepreneur is willing to invest time and money. He knows he will build a successful business for himself and his loved ones—friends, family, children, etc.—over the long term.

- ***Enthusiastically share your products and opportunities every day, and be part of those that have proven themselves.***

In network marketing, there are many ways to increase your revenues and maintain the account you've worked so hard to build. Most techniques and tactics can be learned easily. They are available online, 24 hours a day, 7 days a week.

One of the most important ways to increase the bottom line and sales of network marketing is through the use of product recommendations. Many marketers know that this is one of the most effective ways to promote a certain product.

You must realize this is a matter of presentation. It's a numbers game; whoever makes the most presentations, recruits the most people, forms the biggest team, and earns the most money. You have a responsibility to share products and opportunities with new people every day. Keep up the daily pace of contacting five to ten new prospects to share what you have with them.

If customers or visitors trust you enough, they will certainly trust your recommendations. Be very careful when using this approach. If you start promoting everything by recommendation, your credibility will be diminished. This is especially noticeable when the recommendations are apparently exaggerated and without much merit.

You may mention depreciative qualities about a given product or service sparingly. Rather than losing points for you, this will make your recommendation more realistic and will tend to increase your credibility.

Furthermore, if your visitors are interested in what you offer, they will be more than happy to learn what is good in the product, what is not, and how the product will benefit them.

When you recommend a certain product, there are certain recommendations to remember about how to make it work effectively and to your advantage.

- ***Become the true expert and leader in your field***

Remember this simple equation: price resistance decreases in direct proportion to confidence. If your visitors' sense and believe that you are an expert in your niche, they are more likely to make that purchase. Today, all kinds of products can be found everywhere, so why buy with you? It's confidence in you and your expertise that will make the difference. On the other hand, if you don't have the confidence and assurance to approve of your products, they will probably feel the same way and will look for another product or service that is more credible.

How do you establish this aura of expertise? By offering unique and new solutions, they would go nowhere else. Prove that what you are promoting, works as promised. Post testimonials, "social proof" and leading recommendations from respected and recognized personalities, in related fields, of course.

Don't bluff. It's better to sound discreet and confident than to shout and attract attention. On the other hand, you don't want to appear amateurish and have this thought for your customers and potential customers. It is better to behave in a relaxed and confident manner at the same time.

And remember; prospects aren't stupid. They actually turn to experts and may already know what you know. If you keep your claims with hard facts and data, they would gladly pay hundreds or even thousands of dollars for your products or services. But if you don't, they are smart enough to try to look at your competitors and what they offer.

Before recommending your product, it is recommended that you try the product and support. Do not run the risk of promoting unwanted products and services. Just think how long it took you to build credibility and trust with your visitors. All it will take to destroy it is a big mistake on your part.

If possible, have product recommendations that you trust 100%. Test the product support before you start, to ensure that the people you refer to will not be abandoned when a problem suddenly occurs.

Take a look at your Network Marketing market and the strategies you use. You may not be focusing on the recommendations your products need. Your action plan may not be the only thing that makes your program work.

Decide to improve yourself daily and promise to be better tomorrow than you were today. You must make this a goal for every day. You should read books, sign up for online or offline training, listen to audio, attend events, and advise your sponsor. Create a personal development plan for your life. Your business will only grow as much as you do, which is why personal development is so important in your business.

- *Lead by example and inspire others by your actions*

If you want to develop a great team and succeed in this industry, you have to lead by example at all times, even when no one is watching. Instead of telling people what to do, you show them. That means you have to inspire others with your actions. Do what you want your team members to do. You're constantly prospecting, recruiting and selling in your company.

- ***Work with motivated business partners***

You can't make it, and you can't drag anyone across the finish line. That's not your job. Your job is to support the people who ask for your help. It's not your job to call or motivate anyone. Instead, your job is to help and support motivated people. Your job is to work with those who want to succeed. It's in your best interest to help people get off to a good start, but it's not your job to do everything for them.

- ***Follow your company's rules and regulations***

You read your company's distribution contract and take the time to learn the rules. Once you know the rules, you make sure you follow them at all times. You encourage your team members to do the same. This helps you and your company avoid trouble.

- ***Get involved and stick with one company***

You must realize that success comes down to finding a good business and staying in it for five years or more. This is not a type of business that is quick to get rich. It takes hard work and perseverance to succeed. Find a business that you want to grow in and stay with over the long term.

Network marketing companies often give the impression of a certain lightness by its low start-up costs: you can create a multinational company with only a few hundred Euros, instead of investing capital of thousands or even millions of Euros. No rent, no employees, few charges, no delivery, you concentrate on sales, marketing, and building your network.

Because of this relative ease, many people conclude that it is also simple to make money. However, while network marketing is a type of business that can generate unlimited residual income, it requires just as much effort and is basically a real business like any other.

I see too many distributors who buy the starter pack, work hard for a few months, and give up eventually because they don't get enough results. You have to give yourself time when you start an MLM business. Imagine that you are planting a tree. You're going to water it, prune it, fertilize it, and give it time to grow. You're not going to say to yourself, "It's been 5 months since I planted it and I still can't see it growing! It doesn't work! It's a scam! I'm done!"

Do you know a variety of bamboo of Chinese origin, which grows only 3 cm in 4 years? In the 5th year, this bamboo grows 30 cm per day! In 6 years, bamboo grows 15 m. But if you leave too early, you will never see the day when a bamboo becomes a forest. If you are in a hurry, you can only harvest salads and vegetables that grow fast. Patience and perseverance are essential to building a solid and sustainable business.

- ***Be loyal to your company's products and services whenever possible***

If your company offers a product or service, you use it, even if it costs more than a similar product. You must be "the product of the product" at all times. If you don't have enough faith in your products or services, how can you ask someone else to do it?

So far we have talked about all the "do's" in Network Marketing, now let's look at all the "don'ts"; these are the mistakes I have seen and reviewed in network marketing:

- ***Avoid those most common MLM errors***

Network marketing is one of the most effective and powerful ways to make money online and offline. It allows everyone to make money via the Internet. Because these network marketing programs are easy to reach, easy to set up, and easy to pay commission regularly, more and more people are now willing to work in this type of business.

However, like all businesses, there are many pitfalls in network marketing. How to make some of the most common mistakes will cost marketers a large part of the profits they make on a daily basis. That's why it's better to avoid them than to regret it later.

- **Error number 1: Choosing the wrong partner**

A lot of people want to make money from network marketing as quickly as possible. In their eagerness to be part of one, they tend to choose a product that works. These are the kinds of products that the MLM considers popular. They choose the product, without really thinking about whether they like the product. Obviously, it's not a very wise decision.

Instead of jumping on the bandwagon, try to choose a product that really interests you. For any effort to succeed, you need to take the time to plan and understand your actions.

Choose a product you like. Then research the product to see if it is in demand. It's easier to promote a product you're passionate about than to promote one for profit alone.

- **Error number 2: Joining multiple Network Marketing companies**

Since network marketing companies are very easy to reach, you might be tempted to reach multiple companies that offer different products and try to maximize the revenue you get. On the other hand, you may think that there is nothing wrong and that products complement each other, there is nothing to lose by being part of many MLMs.

Certainly, it is an excellent way to have several sources of income. However, joining several companies and trying to promote them all at the same time will prevent you from focusing on each one.

The result? The maximum potential of your Network Marketing business is not fully exploited and the revenues generated will not be as huge as you initially thought. The best way to achieve a great result is to join a single company that pays a commission of at least 40%. Then do your best to promote your products with enthusiasm. As soon as you see that they are already making a reasonable profit, you may now be able to join another Network Marketing company.

The technique is to do it slowly and surely. There is really no need to rush into products, especially with affiliate marketing. With the way things are going, the future looks bright and it looks like affiliate marketing will stay that long.

- **Error number 3: Not purchasing the product or using the service**

As a distributor, your main objective is to effectively and convincingly promote a product or service and find customers. To achieve this goal, you must be able to convey certain products and services to customers. This makes it difficult for you to do so when you have not tried these things. You will not be able to promote and recommend them convincingly. You also fail to create a desire among your customers to enjoy everything you offer.

Try the product or service personally, before you sign up as a distributor, to see if it delivers what it promises. If you have, then you are one of the credible, living wills aware of its advantages and disadvantages. Your customers will then feel the sincerity and truthfulness in you and this will encourage them to try it for themselves.

Time is of the essence. Take the time to analyze your marketing strategy and check if you are on the right track. If this is done correctly, you will be able to maximize your network marketing program and earn higher profits.

- **Error number 4: Force a prospect to sell a product or even lie to recruit someone**

You need to act like a professional all the time, not like a desperate car salesman. Don't brag about your prowess, don't lie to your prospects about your income, tell them what you think, not what they want to hear, or pressure someone to sign up or buy from you. Yes, you should always sell, but you should never force someone to accept your offer, whether to buy your products or to join your team.

- **Error number 5: Saying or doing wrong about another distributor, a company, or our profession.**

You must never disparage your sponsor, your upline, your company or other companies or distributors in our profession. Never express these thoughts in public. In case of conflict, you settle it with the person in private. Never put yourself in a superior position to criticize someone. Be a network marketing professional and an industry ambassador.

- **Error number 6: Blaming others for your failure or lack of results**

You take 100% responsibility for your network marketing activity. You will never succeed by putting yourself in the position of a victim. You succeed (or fail) depending on your activity and results. You do not blame your sponsor for not helping you. You are a man or a woman and realize that no one cares about your business as much as you do.

There you go. I spent more time talking about network marketing, the job I know best. I hope you find my advice useful and inspiring. If so, take action now!

Do like an ace!

Checklist in 5 minutes on Network Marketing distributors:

Distributors who fail	Successful distributors
⇨ Working alone	⇨ Success with the team

Network Marketing is about teamwork. Only a successful team can lead your business to success. The success of a team depends on the number of distributors who can work independently. The success of some distributors has dizzying ups and downs. They talk a lot of gibberish and hide the truth. It didn't take long for these types of distributors to fail.

My partner met with distributors who are very good at manipulating human nature. They had a taste for clothes and pretended to be successful people. They took advantage of the fear of losing the opportunity to sell products and services that are only good on paper. The good times of these distributors will not last long. Moreover, the result of their lack of vision and their greed for short-term profit is not only the loss of team members but also the loss of confidence in their networks.

An honest distributor will analyze the advantages and disadvantages according to the situation and will take the time to lead his team, teach it how to develop the network, and guide it to develop the correct attitude of the leader. This is also my way of operating. I always say what I have to say, not necessarily head-on, and I have always followed ethics, conscience, and deontology. Sometimes it makes you lose money in the short term, but it will benefit you in the long term.

How about you? What kind of distributor are you?

STEP #14
EXCEL AS A LEADER

- *Your attitude determines your altitude*

Being a leader is above all an attitude and your **attitude** determines your **altitude**. If you can't think like a leader, you have to work on yourself, otherwise, you won't get far.

I have worked in 5 network marketing companies and have 25 years of experience in this sector. I've seen partners who have signed with our team and have not been able to sign up anymore. After a week, I was informed that these partners had signed with another company and they changed companies again afterward. Why did they change companies? Because the grass is always greener elsewhere.

A leader had told me about his experience: he had a distributor who earned $15,000 in 15 days. This colossal success suddenly made him lose his head. Proud as a rooster, he thought he was a leader, but he forgot that it was his sponsor who helped him. He took the stage and was decorated, applauded, and given a standing ovation, but his behavior and his lack of recognition towards his leader were completely at odds with leadership. The distributor did not work to catch up with his status and this glory that did not belong to him caused jealousy.

The worst part of this story is that he himself was also jealous of others, because he only looked at what he didn't have and forgot that he had already received more with direct support from his sponsor. In 5 months, the income of the said distributor dropped sharply and the main reason was because of his envious side.

In the small world of MLM, there are countless similar cases. The leader who told me about his experience was very emotionally affected when he heard gossip about him from the partners he helped. He felt betrayed.

But it's only in the dark hours that we can recognize the qualities of a true leader. Winston Churchill said, **"Success is not final; failure is not fatal, it's the courage**

to continue that counts." When this leader withdrew his help, all the distributors who had enjoyed this ephemeral glory, due to a lack of leadership and solid competence were unable to maintain or sustain their success. A true leader can be beaten and experience ups and downs, probably even more than others. His difference with others is that he gets up, again and again, with his skill and experience, he will always find success, because he knows the recipe.

Donald Trump was a successful entrepreneur before he was elected President of the United States. In 2016, his fortune was estimated at $4 billion. He inherited his father's fortune and went bankrupt many times, but he always managed to regain his income. Why has he always managed to regain his income? Because the rich have a particular mentality and they always come back to some kind of internal thermostat.

The best lesson in leadership is to lead by example. As soon as you start a business and if you want to develop it, the first thing you have to do is to understand everything you have to do in your business and build your expertise in the field. You have to run faster than your partners, otherwise, you can't ask them to do anything. No one will listen to you if they see that you don't do what you say. Otherwise, you will have much more impact.

One of my leaders understood very well the importance of leadership. In 2 weeks, he memorized the presentation and acquired a global knowledge of the products, the compensation plan, and the steps to follow for distributors. He participated in all the events and was always on time, even if he went to bed at 1 a.m. and only slept 4 hours the night before. All of his partners had a stress level that was impossible when they had an appointment with him because they knew that their leader dared to make sacrifices, worked hard, and was also very demanding. Since he set the example, no one dared to say anything or make any excuses.

- *Expand your comfort zone*

A comfort zone is one where you are comfortable and not afraid to do things. If an action scares you, then it's outside of that zone. The more competent you are, the more comfortable you are in various areas, the greater your comfort zone.

Expanding your comfort zone means working on personal development and investing in yourself. Your development is closely linked to your business and this is valid in any type of business.

What is the difference between "getting out of" and "expanding" your comfort zone? Getting out of your comfort zone means that you put yourself in uncomfortable situations to evolve, but some people can't evolve in this situation. Yes, they take little or no risk, and they are petrified when they are out of their comfort zone, unable to function outside their comfort zone as if they can no longer breathe. For these people, it is recommended to "extend their comfort zone" to work differently and dig deeper into their comfort zone. You are showing a different side of yourself. The result, you and your prospects can experience a different you and themselves from different angles and perspectives.

- *Freedom v.s. assistantship*

Each country has its peculiarities and you have to adapt to the mentality of the country when you develop the local market. For example, for me, France is a particularly complicated market for entrepreneurs. I'm not saying it's impossible to succeed in France, otherwise, I wouldn't be writing this book! Of course, it is and there are many examples.

The main reason lies in their mentality—freedom is very important in our beloved country. A French leader follows his partners twice as much as in other countries because they are used to assistance. Yes, they want freedom and been accompanied, which complicates the task. The challenges for the French partners would be, in my opinion, to have the courage, to take the responsibilities, to gain **true freedom, to** develop their expertise, to build the network, and to **become independent.** You won't have real freedom until you can fly away like a big one.

In life, we are in an eternal struggle to expand our comfort zone, for it is in this ceaseless struggle that we will evolve. Who doesn't have an off-peak period or the unexpected, the accidents of life? It is not because we are going through difficult times, that we are destined to live them perpetually. In Chinese, the word "crisis" means "risk" but also "opportunity". A crisis can become an opportunity if you look at it in a positive light.

One of my former leaders was living penniless, housed by an old friend. He refused to apply for social assistance, because he considered that this was not for **"karma", nor did** it correspond to the mentality of a leader. He had already experienced situations a thousand times worse than this and he took this episode as a transition period, the time it took him to requalify his network and rebuild his mindset with positive thoughts. Knowing him, I know that he will soon return to the circle of leaders and he will make his unique voice heard in the marketing world. It's obvious.

You have seen some positive and negative examples of leadership. Now ask yourself the following questions:

- Where are you going to start, if you want to be a leader?
- Is leadership innate or developed?
- What skills are needed if we want to become a leader?
- Are you tired of being a follower?

Characteristics of leaders

A leaser often has these traits:

- **Positive**: He seeks to solve the problem, is action-oriented and focuses on the human relationship. His enthusiasm is the engine of success.

- **Positioning and commitment:** A leader does not passively wait for an opportunity or run after this or that person, on the contrary, he CREATES **the** opportunity and takes it in hand, he positions himself and announces it clearly, he changes the energy of the conversation and he leads the dance: I am - I believe - I see - I do - I have it.

- **Agile**: Followers tend to resist change. Leaders, on the contrary, face them and use the opportunities generated by change.

- **Courageous:** Courage is not the absence of fear, but **moving forward in spite of the fear.**

- **Responsible and independent:** Are you the type of person who does the job, no matter what, or do you depend on others to guide you every step of the way? No one is responsible for your success or failure except you! Positioning yourself as a victim and blaming others for their failures is always easier to work on yourself. Remember that it is up to you to succeed and no one else!

- **Take the risk:** The biggest risk is never to take a risk. Leaders have only two options—master the fight or fight despite defeats.

- **Listening**: Leaders learn to **listen.** All your prospects know their needs, you just have to listen to them.

- **Communication**: Leaders must set an example of open communication—speak with your head, speak truthfully and sincerely.

- **Delegation**: Leaders share responsibility. Instead of giving the order, they lead by example. Leaders encourage the development of others through challenges. They give them new responsibilities and motivate them, also support them in case of failure.

- **Knowledge of others, of self and the situation**: Leaders understand the importance of being open and passionate about knowledge; they know that this attitude will bring them wisdom.

- **Giving**: Giving is the accelerator for a leader to take shape. The difference between a leader and a future leader is that a leader is dedicated to giving the maximum value every day. Start with a small group and do your best to make it succeed and develop the cohesion you want to bring to it.

- **Creating an inspiring vision for the future:** People need a compelling reason to follow your lead, so you need to create and communicate an inspiring vision of the future.

- **Lifelong Learning and Teaching**: Can you start a network marketing business without any training and expect to succeed? Absolutely not! Being an entrepreneur means adding knowledge to your daily life. Apply that knowledge and turn around to teach others. In today's world, you must spend time learning marketing skills so you can use the power of online strategies to recruit more people to introduce your business and products.

- **Be true to yourself:** Have you ever tried to be someone you're not? You need to grow up, but don't fake your identity. Be open or remain authentic, let your personality show through your leadership style.

- *The skills of leaders*

  - **Management**: Setting strategies, processing reports, assisting with marketing, delivery, and service.

- **Recruitment**: Finding qualified partners to develop the business and the network.

- **Training**: If you want to win, you must train; if you want to constant win, you must train accordingly. Participate in seminars and conventions, listen to audios in transportation/your car on marketing and leadership, and read at least 6 books a year on leadership, attitude, and marketing. Imagine and visualize how many people you can help by teaching others something you have learned. You can do this through your blog or video channel so that your message is spread to many people at once.

    Learning, doing, and teaching is the true nature of a successful MLM leader. Always learning new ways of doing things and sharing information with others.

- **Motivation**: Success requires a favorable environment. It's up to you to create a positive and active space in a sustainable way. If you only know how to show that "I am the boss" with little power in your possession, you will be destined for the following scenario: 1. high turnover of your employees, 2. you blame all your employees and your leaders have no morale, 3. if you are still there, the restructuring will take place .

- **Going out into the field**: Some leaders have little or no work since they have achieved their goal, but if you are far from the field, you cannot be a leader well. If you don't practice your art, you can't be the leader of your team.

- **Show the example**: Applicable in all of the above cases. Do what you tell others to do. An action is worth a thousand words!

STEP #15

GOAL SETTING: MEASURE THE DISTANCE BETWEEN YOUR POSTURE AND THE DESTINATION

• *Why setting goals?*

Goal setting in Network Marketing (and in any business) is mandatory for success in your company. Of course, you have to take action based on these objectives.

To be successful, you have to turn your dreams into reality. This is the purpose of goal setting. Goals are the bridge between your right now and your dream destination.

Now, you're probably going to ask yourself the following questions:

- **Why do you set these goals?**
- Why do you want these changes in your life?
- What do you want in life?
- By answering these questions, you will paint a vision of your life that you can turn into reality by setting goals.

• *What is the objective?*

According to Wikipedia, an **objective** in the project management is a goal (or purpose) that has been set and must be achieved through a project[7].

The purpose of goal setting in Network Marketing is to give you a long-term vision of your life and business. Goals help you understand what it takes to achieve your goal and acquire the skills and daily actions to get there.

As you begin to see progress with even small accomplishments towards your goals, your confidence and your ability to take these daily actions grows stronger.

Start with your final goal, help you create a roadmap to reach it. There is no doubt that you will need to expand your comfort zone to accomplish more in your life.

This process is uncomfortable because a habit is never natural until it is well established! Through personal development, I was able to take small steps out of my comfort zone and break down my goals into manageable pieces to help me move forward. How do you manage to devour an elephant? The idea is to eat it piece by piece. Same for the goals. Draw your dream life in 5 years, 10 years from now, then decide what actions will help you get

---

[7] https://fr.wikipedia.org/wiki/Objectif

there, plan in your diary on an annual, monthly, and weekly basis. It's important to have a vision of your goal—clarity is your compass that leads you to your destination.

Are you ever afraid to move on? It's very natural and that's exactly why you have to force yourself to do something different if you want to succeed in network marketing.

I present some goal-setting strategies to help you achieve your vision.

- ***Learn how to build and tell your story (storytelling)***

People often neglect to develop their stories. What story can you start living now in terms of personal achievement, team building, rank progression and growth of your organization? What is your journey and what have you learned along the way?

Whatever your goals, the development of your story should be the first. Your vision is really to become a leader and to become more than what you are now.

That's how you create your legend. Just imagine how your inspiring story will impact your team and the contacts you talk to. Your story can encourage the growth of others and you can create more stories on your path to success.

- ***Developing a customer service culture***

Sometimes network marketing partners are so focused on recruiting for their team and forget how important it is to create a customer service within it.

An important strategy in goal setting is to develop a team that brings clients together and strengthens them. People who use and benefit from the products on an ongoing basis will increase the volume of their referrals.

When you increase your customer base and teach other members of your team to do the same, your own business and your team will grow.

Customers have always been a priority in my own business. If you serve your customers well and your team as well, you can have thousands of customers, many of whom are on monthly Autoship (automatic order). Plus, happy customers love the products and are open to hearing about the company!

By focusing on growing the customer base and teaching others to do the same, rank and revenue comes by itself.

- ***Be precise in defining your objectives***

Your goal should be as specific as possible and avoid generality. If your objective is too vague, it will be difficult to construct the steps to get there.

For example:

Too general - make a lot of money

Specific - earn $1000 per month

The universe doesn't understand what you mean by "a lot", it only knows the number and $1000 or $1 Million makes no difference to it!

Specific objectives are achievable. If you're in the generality, it's like getting on a train without knowing the direction. How do you plan your route if you don't know exactly where you're going?

- ***Measure your goals***

Even if you do everything right, you still need to measure your progress. In the weight loss example, you weigh yourself at a specific time of day to see if you have made any progress.

Darren Hardy writes in his *The Compound Effect*: "Every day, your daily actions will accumulate to reach the larger goal". The basic message of this book is very powerful: small daily actions will lead you to the life you desire or to disaster.

Think about the goals that will require you to grow and help others. Do your current habits serve your purpose or contribute to your vision? What habits can you put in place in your life to help make your goals a reality?

Assess the skills you need to improve the daily actions needed to achieve your vision, and if you feel the need, invest in training or get coached!

STEP #16
BROADEN YOUR IMPACT WITH SOCIAL NETWORKS

When I started working in sales and Network Marketing, there was no internet yet. It was the time of a unique device in the world MADE IN FRANCE—the Minitel. Starting in 2000, the arrival of the internet turned everything upside down and profoundly transformed our working method. My colleagues and I very quickly saw the opportunity that the internet could bring us and we adapted to these revolutionary tools.

If in the 2000s it was websites and blogs that were fashionable, and still exist in the 2010s, what is certain is that the second decade of the 21st century has been largely dominated by social networks. I imagine that most of you have at least one account or have at least heard of Facebook, Twitter, and Instagram. Anyone can post their thoughts for the world to see, and it didn't take long for companies to be captivated by the topic.

- ***Advertising - the new rules of the game***

Social networks are constantly evolving platforms. A few years ago, you could convert "I like" fans from the Facebook Page and reap generous benefits. As soon as social networks have changed their algorithm, the days when marketers could earn fortunes for free (or almost free) are well and truly over.

Today, you can still convert your fans into customers, but you're going to need a budget for advertising, which isn't everyone's expertise. For example, you have to learn how to target well and do A/B testing, let it run for a while, then change just one element to see if you can optimize results. All this takes time and costs money. Afterward, you can be successful for sure, if you are prepared to receive expensive invoices. There are two possibilities;

either you do it yourself or you entrust the job to an internet marketer, an agency, or a community manager. For me, having a presence on social networks means broadening your impact on notoriety - branding. As far as the background work is concerned, nothing has really changed.

- ***Contact-making tool***

When I talk on the phone, I usually stay for a few minutes. It's not like me to keep the conversation going for hours, and that's especially true at work. I consider the telephone as a tool to make contact, to set up an appointment, not to make a presentation. You can't close a sale over the phone; it doesn't mean to be. The same goes for social networks.

I frequently receive requests from friends on Facebook and I accept most of them after consulting their profile. Some are people I know in real life; others are people I met on Facebook, but I don't consider them real friends until I meet them in person. An hour of face-to-face is worth hours of Facebook Messenger. The idea is always the same; don't talk about business right away, never force your hand, otherwise, you'll lose the sale and the relationship. I often receive messages that tell me immediately about their business, even though I hardly know them. If they do, I'll make them understand that dialogue goes both ways, otherwise, it's a monologue and I have something to offer them too. It's never very pleasant to get to the heart of the matter without first establishing a relationship of trust. Real contacts have to be established over time and allow time to put into practice what you have cultivated on social networks. In reality, you can't work with anyone without trust. I prefer to work with competent people, to whom I give my trust. I like to work in a good mood, open-minded and bring a touch of humor to every conversation. I love to bring joy. After all, why do we work? Isn't it to have a better life?

As for the invitation, some marketers recommend making massive additions to social networks. Personally, I do not recommend it, because 1. You risk being considered as spam and being blocked by Facebook. 2. You are too intrusive and if your **desire to** get something from your new friend is stronger than your sincerity to give **value**,

you will scare the person away and you get blocked either by Facebook or by your Facebook "friend".

This does not mean that you should NOT invite friends to Facebook, but rather focus on quality rather than quantity. In line with the Law of Attraction, I make a list on paper of the contacts I would like to have. By doing so, I add friends consciously following the characters cited in this list. This works perfectly for me and I recommend that you do it as well. You will have a better chance of connecting with people who match your aspirations.

- *Choose 1 or 2 platforms and work on them thoroughly*

I have accounts on Facebook, Youtube and LinkedIn. I am not present everywhere on all social networks. Like everyone else, I make posts, watch professionals, make videos, and work with marketers. I like to work in a team and I consider social networks as a marketing department in their own right. I personally manage my Facebook profile and my Facebook Page, with professionally made photos and videos. This is my way of working on social networks, but you don't have to do the same. For me, social network accounts are first and foremost a showcase that shows a lifestyle, a person's philosophy, and character traits. You can manage by yourself like I do, or publish simultaneously on several accounts via software like Buffer, or get a community manager to manage them for you.

- ***Social networks at the service of Network Marketing***

Social networks allow you to contact your audience directly or to reach them via a post. It allows you to build loyalty, develop a brand, and easily obtain testimonials for your company.

Firstly, you should be aware that you have two different target groups; those who know you/your industry and those who do not. This means that your content will cover the whole spectrum and your chances of engagement will increase considerably. To do this, you need to create content that meets the needs of both groups. However, you need to focus most of your social networking efforts on the group that knows you or your industry. By focusing your social activity in this area, you will achieve higher engagement rates through their interest in your messages and understanding of your business.

Secondly, it is recommended that you develop a social media strategy so that your content is consistent. For example, on Mondays, you publish on motivation, on Wednesdays, you publish tips, and on Fridays, you publish facts. The key to social media is to remain consistent with your image, your niche, and your posts. For example, if you are a distributor of an MLM in the health field, all your posts must revolve around your lifestyle (sport, lifestyle...), your leadership, and your company. On the other hand, be careful not to sell your products directly on social networks under your personal account. At this point, your posts are perceived as advertisements and are not well seen. Talk about your services or your products when meeting with your prospects.

It takes time to create a sequel and even longer for the sequel to begin to engage. And don't forget to research current trends on social networks. Keeping up to date with popular trends can really help you grow your network.

Thirdly, you need to create a website. This website is your showcase showing who you are and what you offer. Sometimes a capture page is enough to collect information from prospects and create your own list. You can also create a blog. Starting a blog is a great way to quickly track your online presence, as you can direct your social media subscribers to your blog/website. It also means that you own this traffic and have full control over the content displayed. It also allows you to add data capture elements; perhaps capturing a prospect's email and phone number so you can follow up with them.

Once you have created your site and have visitors on your blog/website, this is where you can start engaging with them on an individual basis, offering them help/advice on your products or services, or you can even start canvassing with anyone who seems interested.

You must take full advantage of the visitors you receive because they share an expressed interest. Something you could do is to film a short introductory video of yourself explaining what you do. Give value, information as a gift. Everybody likes gifts and it's hard to refuse them. Show them how you can help them and what they could gain by joining your network marketing company, you could even ask your team to film short testimonial videos and put them up for review. The general idea of using social media for business is to create audiences and then direct them to an online place where you can control what happens and not face changes in the rules/algorithms of social media companies.

STEP #17

GET CLOSER TO INSPIRING ENTREPRENEURS

- *You are the average of the five people you spend the most time with*

Jim Rohn, a speaker known for his talks on personal development and how to achieve one's dreams and goals, says: "You are the average of the five people you spend the most time with".

I don't know about you, but if I've been able to get to this level, it's probably because of my network which might seem obvious to you because I've worked in Network Marketing for a long time. In reality, every entrepreneur has to be a network man or woman if he or she wants to achieve ambitious goals. "Alone we go faster, together we go further". This African proverb condenses in one sentence the essence of the principle of collective intelligence. According to Wikipedia, collective intelligence refers to the ability of a community to bring together intelligence and knowledge to advance towards a common goal. It results from the quality of interactions between its members[8].

Humans are communal beings. Everyone begins his or her first moments in community life; first in a family with parents and siblings, then at school, then at work.

Very often, in Western societies, we are led to live individually in the mass; each of our lives disconnected from each other, especially in the big metropolises, we can live for years without knowing our neighbor and feeling any discomfort. You probably manage to live this way, however, if you are always working in your corner and think you can develop everything online for your business, you are wrong.

---

[8] https://fr.wikipedia.org/wiki/Intelligence_collective

As my career has evolved, I have met well-known personalities and experts. Unknown at the beginning, little by little, I became the mentor of the world's top leaders in Network Marketing. Today, I have a vast network with whom I keep in touch. What I recommend is to start with a **core**. Create a core and work with competent and trusted people. As you go along, expand that core in a cluster-like fashion and you'll have a great team. Take the time to find good people, because your success depends on the quality of your partners. You first.

- *Tell me whom you're friend with, I'll tell you who you are*

How do you recruit good partners and get to the next level? Having a good network will change your game considerably.

Networking is one of the most important skills you can acquire to make your business a success. Most entrepreneurs believe that they can simply start a business and customers will come. Any successful entrepreneur will immediately tell you that this is not the case.

Building a successful business takes a lot of time and dedication, so it makes sense to have a network of business partners and associates to draw energy and keep you motivated. By surrounding yourself with people who share a similar passion and determination, you are more likely to move forward and get results. Business networking is a valuable way to expand your knowledge, learn from the success of others, gain new customers, and tell others about your business.

A strong and active business network has advantages that can help your business grow and prosper.

What are the main benefits of networking? In my opinion, we can list at least 6:

1. Opportunities

Networking is a user-friendly way to create opportunities. But you won't know when or how they will happen. Networking always offers many opportunities and that is where the benefits of business networking are huge. The opportunities you get involved in should match the vision you have for your business. If they don't, you may find that you pursue opportunity after opportunity without any concrete results.

I have a 30-year-old friend who lives in the South of France, who introduced me to a friend who works in real estate and who is connected with the Chinese. As I know a friend who knows Chinese entrepreneurs, the partnership opportunities came naturally and everyone was a winner. People are looking to sell and I'm just talking about it. That's the power of the network; knowing someone who knows someone who knows someone who and so on. You don't know when opportunities will be created, but you want to be ready when they are. Networking needs to become part of your life and become your habit. If you don't contact your acquaintances regularly and only contact them when you need them, it won't lead to anything concrete.

2. Tips

Networking is a wonderful way to tap into advice and the knowledge that you might not otherwise, have been able to obtain. Having like-minded entrepreneurs also allows you to get advice from them on all sorts of things related to your business or even your personal life and to achieve that important work-life balance. Just make sure you're listening to the right person - someone who really knows what you need to know and isn't just giving you their opinion on something they have little or no experience with.

3. New partnership

This is undoubtedly the most obvious benefit and the reason why most entrepreneurs decide to participate in networking events and join networking groups, masterminds, or clubs such as Country Club or Rotary Club. Through networking, you will establish a professional relationship with other entrepreneurs. Because you will also be networking with others, you will be connected overtime to hundreds or even thousands of people. Through referrals and word of mouth, many of these people have the potential to become future customers. The good news is that the referrals, which you get through networking, are normally of high quality and most of the time are even pre-qualified for you.

5. Branding

Being visible and getting noticed is a huge benefit of networking. By regularly attending business and social events, the company will begin to recognize you. This will help you build your reputation as a knowledgeable, reliable, and supportive person by offering useful information or advice to those who need it. You are also more likely to get more leads and references because you will be the one who will come to mind when they need what you offer.

6. Friendship

Many friendships are formed as a result of networking because you are all like-minded entrepreneurs who want to grow your business. You meet and help each other on a regular basis, so naturally strong friendships tend to form. While this benefit may not be directly applicable to your business, don't overlook the simple advantage of having friends in the business world without any strings attached. You need to know that you have someone to support you that you have people who are there for you.

6. Insider information

I have been in contact with the members of GIN (Global Information Network) founded by Kevin Trudeau and I know members at the highest level. Participating in this type of club gives you access to privileged information because, believe me, valuable information in considerable quantities remains hidden from the general public. You have to know the tips to find them.

- ***Evolve with your network and make it evolve***

Things are impermanent. People will change and your relationships will change as you grow up.

When I went from a stranger to a great leader, I sometimes discovered the other face of my entourage. Normally there are always more people talking than acting. That's why there are only a few people who succeed. Some liked to show their importance, saying that they were inspired by the mentors, and that they saw that I have talent that they would certainly help me. When I was proposing a reciprocal arrangement, sometimes people tended to forget the meaning of the word and focus more on their interests. Some people have accomplished careers and we've always had a good relationship, but when I wanted to boost my career and go to the next level, they pointed out 1001 reasons why I can't do it and I won't succeed. Throughout the conversation, I dug deeper, and I discovered that they weren't where they used to be, and as a result, they didn't have the same power. In reality, they were not in a position to help me, and they avoided revealing it by discouraging me.

Such is human nature; when there is no relationship of interest, many things do not matter. Once fame and fortune are involved, human nature will naturally tilt the balance towards him instead of trying to achieve balance and make his partner benefit as well.

Let's be frank, like a plant, you often have to change "pot" to flourish. Pots that suit other people do not necessarily suit you. If your entourage becomes weeds or if your friends do like those crabs hold back those who try to get out of the bucket, and prevent you from going to the next level, change pot!

Today, I have developed the ability to build an effective network. The president of a large international trade club who has only known me for a few days, talking to me a few times, was ready to offer me interviews and to broadcast the video of the interview in Asian countries through his contacts on the spot. That's the power of the network.

Check your network at any time and improve your capabilities every day. You need your network to help you succeed. Your network will also need you to help it succeed someday. To do this, you need to grow with the times!

DARE TO TAKE FLIGHT

By Robert Ingelaere

If you were on an internship in aviation, what would be the final step that would allow you to concretize your apprenticeship and become a real pilot?

Flying, no doubt.

At the beginning of this book, I told you about my youth, my career as a door-to-door salesperson, and at RCI, the forerunner of Network Marketing.

I've had some phenomenal success stories and some bottomless pits as well. After a burn-out, I went to Thailand to rest and settle down, to find the meaning of life again. The holidays went into overtime - I stayed there for 25 years, married with two children. I was born a *ch'ti* who speaks Northern patois. My work and my life in Thailand lead me to speak English and Thai. My network of professional partners extends to Europe, the United States, Asia, and Africa.

The first glories and setbacks overwhelmed me. Life gave me a gift and I came back, strengthened.

I made € 400 Million in turnover in an MLM, and I repeated the same pattern when I changed companies. In 10 days. Ovations and awards, luxuries and trips to dream landscapes. Everyone chased me, surrounded me, adored me, and idolized me.

I have also experienced lean periods and moments of loneliness. Poverty is scary as well as illness. When you have both, you have to endure the loneliness for a period of time. For three years in a row, I had septicemia, followed by tuberculosis and diabetes. I was dying, I was losing weight in the daytime; the Thai villagers said I was going to die. While I was struggling between life and death, those people who used to chase after me, surround me, worship me, and idolize me, disappeared. In the descent into misery and decadence, at times I was forced to choose between sleeping or eating: either I slept almost on the floor on a cheap mattress with a bad back all the time, or I ate an industrial or fast food meal once a day; I was so hungry that I felt like I was going back to my adolescence. People were so used to having me paying for everything when I was rich, that they couldn't understand when I ran out of money, I couldn't help it.

The high-level leader may be alone when you reach a certain height because your peers are rare at this level. I have traveled all over Europe and the world; I have also been bedridden because of health problems. I've taken a beating but it doesn't matter. The main thing is that I found solutions and let go, to free myself from the burdens I had carried. Life goes on and I move on.

Charles Aznavour sings in "*I Could See Myself Already.*"

When I was eighteen, I left my province...

Determined to seize life

The light heart and the thin luggage

I was sure I would conquer Paris

At the chicest tailor's I've had made...

That blue suit that was the latest thing

Photos, songs, and orchestrations

Went through my savings.

That's a bit of my story, this provincial who came to Paris to fulfill his dream: "*Others succeeded with little voice and a lot of money/I was too pure or too ahead of my time/But one day I'll show them that I've got talent.*"

Yes, I'll come back, and *I'll show them that I'm talented*. I've never given up after all I've been through; I know I'm on the right path. I am a survivor, a country that is resurrecting after the war, and I want to live every moment intensely to enjoy the gifts of life.

You too, from the moment you decide to become an entrepreneur, you will go through not one, but several areas of turbulence. Will your business survive after violent storms and jolts?

I like to be an entrepreneur and I like to make things big. I want to be the best or nothing. If we all have this opportunity to live an extraordinary life, why settle for mediocre? Why be small when you can be big? This chance is given to everyone and is just waiting for you to welcome it. Don't settle for what you have. Aim for excellence in your field of expertise, and access the pleasures of your accomplishment.

This book is written for you. You, who want to be a successful entrepreneur.

Fly, cross turbulent areas, go for your success, dare to take flight.

Fly to the top! We're waiting for you there.

DUO ACKNOWLEDGEMENTS

By Ling-Chih and Robert Ingelarere

Ling-Chih:

This book was born in a setting curiously similar to my first "A Binary Star": they were both made during a coaching session. If the idea to write the story of "A Binary Star" did not come from me, "The Paradox of Success" was born in the joy of having discovered a gold mine and I know by instinct that the story needs to speak. To achieve this, the realization took shape in hard work and I naturally integrated Robert's coaching teaching, because it is the fruit of all these years of experience.

This book was written in French and this choice came naturally because Robert is French and our reader is above all French-speaking. We would like this book to be published in other languages and help readers in other countries who are looking to develop their business online or offline.

Thanks to my mentor Robert Ingelaere; when I made the joke, I never thought it would come true! You inspired me and made me want to write your story. Even if it's no longer a biography, this book has something of you in it. Thank you so much for your trust and I understood that you were pushing me for a vision. A leader is a visionary: "*I already saw myself*[9]"!

Everything starts from a thought and everything is faithful to the law of attraction: **what I want, wants me**[10]. I find it very beautiful that when I came up with the idea of

---

[9] Title of a song by Charles Aznavour.

[10] Rûmî, the 13th century poet, expresses the same insight in the following verses: "When I run after what I think I want, my days are a source of stress and anxiety; if I sit in my own place of patience, what I need flows towards me without difficulty. From this, I understand that what I want also wants me, seeks me and attracts me. There is a great secret here for anyone who can understand it."

making a book out of it, this book was already waiting for me and that I was writing it so that it could take shape.

Robert Ingelaere:

Let's go back to what I mentioned at the beginning of the book, in "Success is a state of mind", I created my legend. Now it's up to you to create yours. You certainly have a role to play and you are in this world to shine. We would like this book to help you rise.

In business, there are actors and carriers. Thanks to the carriers, the actors can go further and make their dreams come true. The carriers, in turn, can be actors. The beauty of the thing is when we carry each other upwards.

For this, we would like to thank all those who helped us with the publication of this book.

Thanks to Isabelle Calkins for your precious advice on the photo and the title. Thanks to Rachel Etchevarne, David Pothin, Anna Reda, Patricia Bounzel, Laurent Gousset, and Doris Guo for the proofreading.

Thank you to all those who made this book possible!

ANNEX I

ENTREPRENEURIAL OR SALARIED? A CHECK-UP TO FIND OUT WHICH SIDE YOU'RE ON

Is there a way to determine if you can be a successful entrepreneur or if you are destined to work for someone else? Unfortunately, there is no formula for success. However, most successful entrepreneurs have these 10 points in common. Check out how many you have:

- ***Think of success***

To achieve the kind of success you want, you have to dream big. Every success story begins with big dreams. You have to dream big for yourself -- to become rich, successful in your business, and fulfilled. According to the Law of Attraction, building a great palace is just as easy as building a bridge to the Universe. It is humans who limit themselves by telling themselves that this or that is impossible.

You need to have a clear vision of what you want to achieve, and that doesn't stop at dreaming alone. You should actively visualize success in your mind that you can almost feel it, touch it or that it is within your reach. Play this image at every opportunity. How does it feel to triple your current income? How will your life change? What will your business look like if you reach the million-dollar mark?

Successful entrepreneurs have an attitude of openness and trust; you can have what you want if you can simply see it as the first step on the road to acquiring it. Spirituality teachers and coaches have taught us the power of visualization -- seeing yourself in your mind as having fulfilled your dreams. If you want to be a successful writer, imagine signing books for a crowd of people who lined up to get your autograph. If you want to be rich, imagine yourself in a luxurious environment with a big bank account. And the process of success envisioned for you should be a constant activity! Think about being successful as often as possible, especially at bedtime, and when you get out of bed.

A personal development coach confided in me her secret to help her visualize her goals at all times; when you climb stairs, recite your goal at every step. So, if you want more money, say "I'll have money" at every step of the stairs. This technique will reinforce your goal and keep it fresh in your mind.

- ***Be passionate about what you do***

You are starting a business to change all or part of your life. To achieve this change, you must develop or discover an intense personal passion: to change the current situation and live life to the fullest. Success comes easily if you love what you do. Why is that? Because we are more relentless in the pursuit of goals for things we love. If you hate your job now, do you think you'll ever succeed? Not in a million years! You can make it work and even become proficient at it, but you'll never succeed. You will perform at your best and only do what you need to do to succeed if you do something that interests you or is important to you. Successful entrepreneurs are not embarrassed by the fact that they spend 15 to 18 hours a day on their business because they love what they do. Success in business depends on patience and hard work, which can only be achieved if you are passionate and crazy about your tasks and activities.

- *Focus on your strengths.*

Let's face it, you can't be everything to everyone. Each of us has our strengths and weaknesses. To be effective, you need to identify your strengths and focus on them. You will be more successful if you can focus your efforts on the areas you do best. In business, for example, if you know you have good marketing instincts, exploit that strength and use it to the fullest. Ask for help or training in areas where you might be weak, such as accounting or bookkeeping. To turn your weakness into a strength, consider taking a hands-on apprenticeship or formal training.

- *Never consider the possibility of failure*

As an entrepreneur, you must fully believe in your goals and be able to do so. Think that what you do will contribute to the improvement of your environment and yourself. You should have great confidence in your idea, your abilities, and yourself. You should believe without a shadow of a doubt that you can recognize and fulfill them. The more you can develop for confidence in your ability to achieve your goals, the sooner you will be able to achieve them. However, your confidence must be balanced with the calculated risks you must take to achieve greater rewards. Successful entrepreneurs are those who analyze and minimize risk in the pursuit of profit. As they always say, "No courage, no glory."

- *Plan in consequence*

Do you have a vision and do you know how to achieve your vision? To achieve your vision, you need to have concrete goals that will be a stepping stone to your ultimate vision. Write down your goals; don't make them just intangible fantasies. You need to plan each day so that every action is taken to achieve your vision. Perhaps today you will need to see an artist to help you conceptualize the new line of linens you hope to launch. Intense goal orientation is the hallmark of every successful entrepreneur. They have a vision and they know how to get there. Your ability to set goals and plan your realization is the required ability for success. Plan, plan and plan - otherwise failure is guaranteed.

- ***Love your work, passionately, madly!***

Every successful contractor works hard, very hard. No one succeeds just by sitting and looking at the wall every day. The great Brian Tracy said, "You work eight hours a day to survive; anything more than eight hours a day is a success. "Ask any successful and prosperous businessman, and he'll tell you right away that he has to work more than 60 hours a week when he starts his business.

Be prepared to say goodbye to bars after work every day or a regular weekend. If you're in a start-up phase, you'll need to breathe, eat and drink your business until it can run on its own. Working hard will be easy if you have a vision, clear goals and are passionate about what you do.

- ***Constantly look for ways to network***

In business, you are judged by the company you keep - by your management team, your board of directors and your strategic partners. Often, you will find help from resources outside the company. Perhaps the lady you met at a trade association meeting can help you get funding, or the gentleman at a conference can provide management advice. It is important to form alliances with people who can help you and who you can help in return. To succeed in business, you need good networking skills and always be on the lookout for opportunities to expand your contacts.

- **_Willingness to learn_**

You don't need to have a Havard or a PhD diploma to be successful in your own business. In fact, many entrepreneurs have not even completed high school. Studies show that most self-confident millionaires have average intelligence. Nevertheless, these people have reached their full potential and have achieved their financial and personal business goals because they are willing to learn. To succeed, you must be willing to ask questions, remain curious, interested and open to new knowledge. This willingness to learn is becoming more crucial with the rapid evolution of technology and work methods.

- **_What if I still can't make it, and I'm no longer enjoying what I'm doing?_**

My answer may surprise you: Forget it.

Yes, it is as simple as that. I know I am talking about the importance of perseverance throughout the book, and all the coaches, society, inspirational films encourage you to insist, never give up. And it is true, if you have faith and enthusiasm in what you do, and your company always pleases you, then persevere. Otherwise, stop, cease fighting for something you don't believe because it is a waste of time. It is not a joke. Life is short, and if you do not enjoy it fully, what is the point? Maybe you are not cut out for it, and you certainly have other talents. Sometimes it is a matter of timing, you will never know, maybe someday you will have *Kensho*[11] moment, and you will come back one day.

One of my students spent 8 years in an industry without any real success. He stayed in this sector because his leaders told him never to give up. "No matter how long it takes, we'll get there someday." But I can see that he doesn't believe in it deep down, and that he's ashamed of the work. I made him understand that his talent lies elsewhere. Today, he is more fulfilled. What's happened? ~~Because he has found his~~ way. Sometimes letting go for

---

[11] **Kensho** (Japanese) is a term used in Zen traditions meaning "seeing into one's true nature. " Ken means "seeing," sho means "nature" or "essence. " Satori and kensho are commonly translated as enlightenment, a word that is also used to translate bodhi, prajna and buddhahood.

https://jisho.org/word/%E6%82%9F%E3%82%8A

the right reasons is a wise decision. There's no shame in that, and success doesn't only belong to the young. We still have the opportunity to grow even in middle age. It's a cliché, but all you really need to do is open up and be willing to start the process of change.

ANNEX II
COACHING WITH ROBERT INGELAERE

Discover Robert Ingelaere

The principles of success of the company are proven.

You will learn,

What unique traits of most successful entrepreneurs have in common

How to organize your time and attention and invest well in your business

How to identify and eliminate the habits that prevent your success

Specific strategies, harvested directly from life, which proved to be the main difference between those responsible for failure and success

---

I was used to only reserving my free coaching for my leaders.

Today, I offer two coaching options to those who wish to do so, either **face-to-face or online**.

Face-to-face coaching corresponds to the individual need, each one being unique.

I propose a rare offer: I accompany you until the results are achieved. If you know the coaching market, you surely know that coaching often lasts a few months and that there are no guarantees. I cannot guarantee how long it will take you to reach your goal, but I can guarantee you my presence until you succeed! And this, with the participation of a team set up in the following areas:

- Sound
- Branding coaching
- Speech
- Marketing

To help our partners succeed.

Online coaching has the merit of democratizing teaching by making it more affordable. You can follow it at any time. More information is coming soon. Thank you for following me on:

Facebook Page: https://www.facebook.com/LaLettreRobertIngelaere/

Linkedin: https://www.linkedin.com/in/robert-ingelaere-05873323/

Robert Ingelaere

Testimonials:

Elodie, creator of a cosmetics brand: "I had a lot of trouble getting myself known and bringing in customers. Robert helped me to create new partnerships. Thanks to him, I quickly became a referral and stood out from the crowd."

Ling-Chih, translator and writer: "Robert's coaching enabled me to sign five professional contracts in the first month. Never seen this before in my life!"

NOTES

1. Rhonda Byrne, *Le Secret,* Un monde différent, 2008

2. Esther Hicks & Wayne W. Dyer, *Co-creating at Its Best: A Conversation Between Master Teachers,* Hay House, 2014

3. Esther & Jerry Hicks, *Demandez et vous recevrez*, Ariane Éditions Inc., 2006

4. Napoleon Hill, *Think and Grow Rich* (the original unedited 1937 text), Napoleon Hill Foundation, 2017

5. Centre national du livre : « Les Français et la lecture en 2019 » https://centrenationaldulivre.fr/donnees-cles/les-francais-et-la-lecture-en-2019

6. Fredrik Eklund et Bruce Littlefield, *The Sell: The Secrets to Selling Anything to Anyone*, Penguin Random House, 2015

7. Ken Honda, *Money EQ* on Mindvalley.com, 2020

8. Elizabeth Gilbert, *Big Magic*: Creative Living Beyond Fear, Riverhead Books, 2016

9. Jeffrey H. Gitomer, *The Sales Bible: The Ultimate Sales Resource,* William Morrow and Company, Inc.

10. Rich Karlgaard, *Late Boomers: The Power of Patience in a World Obsessed with Early Achievement*, Currency, 2019

11. Michael Ellsberg, *The Education of Millionaires*, Portfolio/Penguin, 2011

12. Dr Michael Breus, *Quand?*, Belfond, 2017

SUMMARY

THE PARADOX OF SUCCESS	1
GENESIS OF THIS BOOK	8
SUCCESS IS A STATE OF MIND	15
PREAMBLE	18
PART ONE:	27
SUCCESS IS A DECISION AWAY	27
STEP #1	29
THE MINDSET OF THE DOOR-TO-DOOR SALESMAN AND SUCCESSFUL MARKETERS	29
STEP #2	45
KEEP THE MOTIVATIONAL FLAME BURNING NO MATTER WHAT HAPPENS	45
STEP #3	52

ATTRACT ABUNDANCE INTO YOUR LIFE AND THINK UNLIMITEDLY	52
STEP #4	60
PART TWO:	65
HOW TO DEVELOP, CREATE NEEDS, NEGOTIATE	65
STEP #5	67
BRANDING: BUILD YOUR PERSONAL BRAND	67
STEP #6	75
THE EDUCATION OF MILLIONAIRES	75
STEP #7	84
YOU WANT TO BE THE BOSS? THEN BECOME THE EXPERT IN YOUR FIELD!	84
STEP #8	105
THE ART OF PERSUASION	105
STEP #9	110

DEVELOP YOUR SUPER BRAIN	110
STEP #10	116
KNOWING WHAT YOU REALLY WANT AND SETTING GOALS	116
STEP #11	121
CLOSING OR HOW TO GET A SALE	121
STEP #12	133
ORGANIZATION OF TIME	133
PART THREE:	139
REJOICE IN WHAT SALES AND MARKETING CAN BRING TO EVERYONE - IT'S ALSO A LIFESTYLE!	139
STEP #13	141
NETWORK MARKETING: A TURNKEY BUSINESS	141
STEP #14	173
EXCEL AS A LEADER	173

STEP #15 186

GOAL SETTING: MEASURE THE DISTANCE BETWEEN YOUR POSTURE AND THE DESTINATION 186

STEP #16 194

BROADEN YOUR IMPACT WITH SOCIAL NETWORKS 194

STEP #17 203

GET CLOSER TO INSPIRING ENTREPRENEURS 203

DARE TO TAKE FLIGHT 214

DUO ACKNOWLEDGEMENTS 219

ANNEX I 222

ENTREPRENEURIAL OR SALARIED? A CHECK-UP TO FIND OUT WHICH SIDE YOU'RE ON 222

ANNEX II 232

COACHING WITH ROBERT INGELAERE 232

NOTES 236

www.ingramcontent.com/pod-product-compliance
Lightning Source LLC
Chambersburg PA
CBHW071355210526
45465CB00001B/97